Shamanism for Teenagers, Young Adults and the Young at Heart

Shamanic practice made easy
for the newest generations

Shamanism for Teenagers, Young Adults and the Young at Heart

Shamanic practice made easy
for the newest generations

Robert Levy

Winchester, UK
Washington, USA

First published by Soul Rocks Books, 2014
Soul Rocks Books is an imprint of John Hunt Publishing Ltd., Laurel House, Station Approach,
Alresford, Hants, SO24 9JH, UK
office1@jhpbooks.net
www.johnhuntpublishing.com
www.soulrocks-books.com

For distributor details and how to order please visit the 'Ordering' section on our website.

Text copyright: Robert Levy 2013

ISBN: 978 1 78279 449 3

A CIP catalogue record for this book is available from the British Library.

Design: Lee Nash

Printed in the USA by Edwards Brothers Malloy

We operate a distinctive and ethical publishing philosophy in all
areas of our business, from our global network of authors to
production and worldwide distribution.

CONTENTS

Acknowledgment

To Aimee Morgana, who for many years kept suggesting that I write a shamanic book for teenagers.

You were my first shamanic teacher. It was because of your patience, your understanding, your teachings, and your smile that I took my first steps into the shamanic world. It was because of you this book was written. It was because of you that my first spirit guide appeared, and together, we began the journey I am still on.

You were most generous with your time, your efforts and, most of all, your faith and belief in me. Not in the me I was, but the me you knew I could become. With your help, I think I have become that person.

May your doors and gates be forever open, and may the doors and gates of those who wish you any ill be forever closed.

To my wife, Shigeko,
You make me keep writing books
So I can tell the world
How much I love you!

Author's Note: The techniques explained in this book are for informational purposes only. They are not meant to replace any health care professional.

In the memory of Ipupiara Makunaiman, who along with his wife Claicha Toscano was the first who named me shaman and who taught me how to claim the title by believing in myself.

Shamanic Basics

The name of this book is *Shamanism for Teenagers, Young Adults and the Young at Heart*. It was written for one purpose – to help you begin walking a shamanic path in the simplest way possible. When I began my walk in 1995, my beginning was anything but simple. I don't want you to stumble over the rocks and obstacles I did. I want to empower you. I want you to achieve whatever dreams you have for your future, regardless of your age. I want you to say to yourself with power, conviction and self-confidence after completing the exercises in this book, "I am a shamanic practitioner." And I promise, you will be.

I'm going to keep it simple and will not clog your mind with things you don't need to know now. There are enough things adults around you want you to know and you probably don't want to know them anyway. Keeping it simple doesn't mean adults can't read this book – they can if they wish. This is a 'how to' book, and if adults want to learn the same things you do in the easy way I plan to teach you, they can. It may just be more difficult. If you are wondering why it will be harder for them the answer is simple. Adults are old, and the older they are, the harder it will be no matter how simply I write. That's because many times adults may have forgotten how to believe in their imaginations. I know I did.

I said may because not all of them have forgotten. They, like you, have a dream and are willing to do what they have to in order to achieve it. To those readers who fit into that category, welcome! If you are young at heart with a youthful soul that wants to fly, come and join us as we begin to demystify the ageless secrets of becoming a shaman. And if you have had any difficulties in the past trying to stay on a shamanic path, come with us too, and those difficulties will soon be solved.

Let's begin with, "Who most of you may be?" You are a young

person who has heard or read something about shamans and it intrigued you. Maybe you saw a movie about a shaman and might have felt chills racing up and down your back as you watched magic happen on the screen. And being a teenager struggling with who you are and what you want life to give you, you also wondered if you too could be a shaman and do that kind of magic. I call myself a shamanic practitioner; a person who practices shamanism, and my answer to you is yes you can. But it is a qualified yes. You can become a shaman, a shamanic practitioner, and you can and will be able to experience the magic of being one. But you won't be able to do the magic you saw in the movies. In our world, you won't be able to turn into a bird and fly away; but in the shaman's world, you will be able to speak to the bird, merge with it and become part of it. Then you will experience how it feels to fly when the bird does. When you have learned more about the alternate reality of the shaman and are within it, you will become the bird yourself and experience flying on your own.

First, let's define shaman and begin to tell you how you start your journey to become one. Shamanism is a personal journey you want to take in order to help you live a better life by knowing yourself better. A shaman, or shamanic practitioner, is a person who allows her/his mind to travel into the spirit world. That's where the spirits like that of the bird you may meet live. The reason people enter that other or alternate reality is in order to find one or more of several things. The three most important things you may find in the beginning are:

Information or knowledge about things you need or want to know about yourself and guidance about how to use that information to help you solve a problem you are having.

Wisdom, very difficult even for many adults, that may help you understand why the problem exists in the first place and what you need to do to solve it.

2

Power, not the kind that will turn you into a super hero, but the personal power that will give you the strength to do what you feel you must in order to solve the problem.

Now this is a very simple definition of what a shaman does. There are many other aspects of being a shamanic practitioner in our world, but in the beginning, learning to be with and communicating with spirit is the most important. I told you, you have enough in your mind now and I will not put more into it unless you need to know it. And you don't need to know more about becoming a shaman now. As you continue walking the shamanic path, as you continue to learn to stretch and strengthen your shamanic muscles, you will learn about all the other things shamans do. And if I don't tell you, your spirit guides will. Eventually, they will become your main teachers.

You may have also noticed that my definition of shaman centered on you. This is because many of the roles included in being shamans are closed to us. For example, indigenous shamans are healers and know the healing properties of the plants that grow in their community. They know how to use those plants as medicine. Many times members of the local community go to their shamans for both physical and psychological problems. Shamans can be asked to act as judges, mediating problems for others in their community. These roles are impossible for us to copy. Therefore I have limited my definition to the most important requisite for being a shaman: being able to communicate with the spirit world. That I know I can teach you how to do.

Getting to the spirit world is easy and I will explain how you do that in a minute. After entering that world and finding the answer to why you went there in the first place, you will then return to our world, our reality and try to do what is necessary to use that information in order to make some kind of change in yourself or the world around you.

You should know this though, and it's very important. You will learn to meet your spirit guides and have them become part of your life, if you wish. But they will not do anything for you in our world. They don't live here; they can't change anything here. They will give you ideas and suggestions about what you can do to solve your problems, but you are the one who has to decide if you will accept those suggestions. That idea is called Free Will, and it simply means spirit will tell you possible solutions, but the actions you take in our reality are solely up to you. Spirit will never say you have to do this. It will only suggest. And the wonderful thing is that all the spirits you encounter will be completely loyal to you. If you don't do as they might suggest, if you don't visit them for a long time, if you do something you think they may not approve of, it doesn't matter. They will always be there for you whenever you go to them. Period.

Now, how do you get to the spirit world? The power that fuels a shaman, what gets them to that world, is called a shamanic journey. This is the way you will enter spirit's reality. You did this many times when you were younger and probably do it now, even though you have no idea you do. A shamanic journey is the easiest thing in the world. Some adults have trouble journeying because they refuse to believe how simple it is. When I started my shamanic path, I was just like those adults. It took me 3 or 4 months to begin to journey. You see, I was very stubborn about not believing. Children, on the other hand, especially young children, 4, 5, or 6 year olds, have no trouble believing. Every time they play pretend or imagine themselves on other worlds or having conversations with invisible people or animals, they are journeying. My former teacher said, "We are all Shamans." And he was right. But I, like most others, forgot we were.

What is a shamanic journey? It's allowing yourself to go into a very light trance and allowing your mind to be free to go where it will in order to find the spirits. All you have to do is tell your mind to go to the spirit world and it will take you. And how do you enter this light trance that takes you there? You close your eyes and daydream yourself being there. It's that simple.

Before I go on, I need to say this. Regardless of what you may have heard or read or have been told, drugs, legal or not, are not part of the shamanic journey. During a journey, you are always in control of who you are. A journey has nothing to do with taking something, hypnosis or not being able to control your body. If you are in the middle of a very deep journey and the fire alarm goes off, you will get up immediately to see what's happening.

A shamanic journey is nothing more than a non-directed daydream. That means, in the beginning, you are going to use your imagination and direct your daydream, experiencing it the way you experience all the daydreams you have ever had before this. The only difference is at some point you will stop directing the daydream and allow it to continue. And it will continue. The daydream you began will soon have a life of its own, and when that happens, you will just follow the daydream and go wherever it takes you. Then, you will be journeying. You'll be like a stick that has fallen into a river, going wherever the current takes you.

I hope you understand now why I say those young children I just spoke of and you, the reader, already journey. The younger you are, the more daydreams you have. The older you are, the less you have.

Why do you have to journey? It is the only way you can enter the spirit world.

How long is a journey? I can't tell you because it's up to you. In a shamanic workshop, the leaders decide how long the journeys last. They drum for the people who are lying on mats or on the floor journeying; and when the leaders change the beat, they are calling everyone back to our reality. But when you are lying in your room, you will decide how long it should be. Usually, when you have enough information about why you took your journey, you can end it. Once you begin to journey, the information spirit gives you will come into you very rapidly. A ten-minute journey is usually long enough.

What should you expect from a journey? To be very honest, my answer is nothing. I don't mean nothing will happen; I mean you should not have any expectations about what will happen. The best way to approach a shamanic journey is with an open mind – with the attitude of what happens will happen. Most of the time, whatever happens will be just what spirit wants to happen.

I have been using the words spirit and spirits since the first page. Regardless of what you think the word spirit may mean (ghosts, walking dead or zombies), let me give you the shamanic definition. Everything in this world has a spirit and you can visit those spirits in the alternate reality any time you want. I'm not only talking about those who are deceased. Though their spirits are alive in that reality and you can journey to them, you should know that in shamanism everything has a spirit. The trees, the flowers, the wind, the rocks, the animals and birds, the insects, the sun, the moon, the rain, the mountains and the clouds all have spirits. Anything else you can point to or call its name has a spirit. Even you have one – I call it your higher self, and I don't mean your soul. Many people define soul in religious terms and shamanism is NOT a religion. But you can go and visit your spirit, your higher self, if you want to. Later you will learn how, and hopefully you will want to.

Remember, you are going to journey to get knowledge (information), wisdom or personal power. In the beginning, what might be a little difficult for you is usually 100 times harder for adults. What is so hard for adults to believe is that even though they began the journey by using their imagination, the spirits that they will meet and the knowledge, information, wisdom and power they will get will be real. When you journey, whatever information you get will be your truth, your reality. It is that truth that will help you with whatever problem you have. Without believing in your truth, there can be no action. Without action, nothing will change. Change does not begin from a source outside your own body. If you wish to change anything about yourself, it must start from within you. And that is not easy. You may, as I did, as adults always do especially when they are beginners, ask yourself, "Is this journey real or is it my imagination?" The answer is it doesn't matter. What matters is what you believe and how you react. The journey comes from within you, from within your mind. The imagination comes from within you, from within your mind. They are the same. It sounds simple but it is the major hurdle most people have to jump over before they can call themselves shamanic practitioners.

This is the last bit of talking before I start telling you how to begin. A shamanic belief that seems to be worldwide is that the spirit world is divided into three parts. The bottom part, where the animal spirits live, is called the Lower World. The middle part, or Middle World, is where we live. It's our world. The top part is called the Upper World and that is where the human spirits live. Now that I have told you, pay no attention to what I just said. Spirits do as they wish and go where they want, and you can search for them in any of the three worlds.

I said a couple of pages ago let's start. So let's start. I think the hardest thing for you to do right now may be to find a place where you can spend alone time, turn off the phone (sorry, it's a must), turn the light down or shut it off, sit in a chair, lie on a couch, a bed, the floor, whichever you want. Just be comfortable and be able to close your eyes.

I'd like you to read what I want you to do, then, when I ask you, close the book and wait until you have done the journey before continuing to read. In the beginning, I would always like you to do the journey before moving on in the book. After 4 or 5 journeys, when you will probably feel more comfortable visiting the spirit reality, you can stop that practice and journey whenever you wish. The reason for asking you to journey before continuing is if you just read most of the book without doing the journeys, everything may sound as if I'm taking you to the Land of Oz. It may not make sense to you, or you may begin to believe that not only am I but all shamanic practitioners are completely crazy. I promise you, we're not.

You need to be in a quiet place. Most shamans and shamanic practitioners believe, and I agree, listening to a drum while you journey is the easiest aid you can use to help reach you to the spirit world. But you don't have to buy a shamanic drumming CD now and wait until you receive it to start journeying. You could go to iTunes or Amazon, search under shamanic drumming and download. (They should all be the same so select the cheapest.) If you get a drumming CD, don't expect a rhythm band. Shamanic drumming is supposed to be monotonous – it's beat, beat, beat, beat. If you were to tap your hand on top of your desk and keep the same 1–2, 1–2, 1–2, 1–2 beat for 10 minutes, you would be doing shamanic drumming. But if you want an alternative, you could listen to any meditative music you like – but it has to be soft and quiet, instrumental not vocal. You don't want anything that will make you stop journeying and start listening to the music. You want to relax your mind. (I understand being who you are may make that difficult. But try!) Go to the iTunes store and if they have music by Anugama, Kamal, Ken Davis, Paul Lloyd Warner, listen to the 10 seconds of music they allow you to, and maybe you'll find one you think you'll like. Or just search for New Age Music and download a few instrumental songs.

When you begin, you're going to close your eyes and start daydreaming. In the beginning, I want you to start every journey the same way.

You are going to look for an animal guide. Usually, your guide has been waiting for you all your life. All you have to do is show up and call out. She or he will usually come.

Since animal guides usually stay in the lower world, that's

where you're going to start, and to get to the lower world, you have to go down to it. But, I'm not going to tell you how to get there. I will tell you some of the ways many shamanic practitioners use to enter the spirit world. As you read, if you say to yourself, "I'm going to try that way first," then that's the one you start with.

Before you start, think of it this way. Shamans have 2 selves. The first self is the bodyself. (I made that word up.) That's the part of you that doesn't go anywhere. It stays right where you are and will be there when you return from your journey. It's the part with your arms and legs, chest and head. The bodyself always stays in our reality, our world.

The second self is the mindself. (I made that word up, too.) That's the part of your brain that holds your imagination, the part that lets you daydream. Not just shamanic daydreams, but all of your daydreams. Any time you think about being somewhere else or in a far off place where people will understand you better, or you close your eyes and really see behind those closed lids anything that makes you feel better, you are using your mindself. When you journey, you are going to send that mindself out (by just starting your daydream) and letting it go wherever it wants.

Journey I

Find Your Guide

Your mindself needs a little help in knowing it has to go down into the earth, and keep going until it comes out in the lower world. That world will look very much like ours – and most people find themselves in a place of nature, a forest or woods, a meadow, a desert, a mountain or even on a beach. And though many people find similar landscapes, you ought to know that what awaits you will be yours and no one else's. Your spirit world will be unique to you because everything you find will be there for one reason: to help you accomplish what you want.

The classic way to reach the lower world is to daydream yourself standing in a natural setting or any place that makes you feel safe and comfortable. Imagine yourself looking around for a natural hole. It could be a hole in a tree, or a space between a rock and the soil. If it is a place you are familiar with in your real world, that's fine. If not, don't worry about it. If you decide to daydream being on a beach, bend down and dig a hole in the sand. What it is doesn't matter as long as it is the tiniest of openings. Now imagine you are shrinking, getting smaller and smaller until the tiny space in the ground is big enough to jump into. Then jump into it and just imagine going through the earth until you come out. Don't concern yourself about imagining growing big again. That will happen automatically by the time you reach the lower world.

Part of the classic way is to imagine that you are standing in a cave. If that appeals to you, try it. You don't have to shrink. If you have ever seen a real cave, imagine yourself in front of it. If you have never seen one, imagine what a cave entrance might look like tucked into the bottom of a mountain. In either case, just walk in. There will always be enough light to see by, and if not, you can always imagine the light getting brighter. All you do is keep walking until you come out the other end. Usually the path will slope downward and you'll never have to get on your hands and knees and crawl. When you reach the end, you'll be in the lower world.

How you get there is not important. Getting there is the main objective. If you don't see a cave, wherever your mindself takes you as you go down is just what you need. You may sense yourself going through solid rock. Keep going until you come out. You may drop out of the sky. If you do and you see a forest below, float down. How? Imagine it. If you float down and land on a mountaintop or in a desert, that's fine too.

Getting to the lower world if you live in a city is not a problem. Daydream that you are in your favorite mall or department store. Get on a down escalator and when you get to the bottom, imagine it and you continuing to go down right through the floor! When it eventually stops, you will be in the Lower World. Or, if there is an elevator in your building, see yourself getting into it and pushing a button that says LW (lower world). The button will be just under the button for the first floor. Daydream the door closing, and when it opens, you too will be in the lower world. Another way people enter is just imagining jumping into the crack in a sidewalk.

If you like the water, here's a watery entrance. Daydream yourself standing on the top of a waterfall and dive off it. When you imagine hitting the water, keep going down and through the ground under the water. When you come out, you're in the lower world.

What is your favorite hobby? Whatever it is, there has to be some part of it that you can imagine yourself doing and seeing the smallest of openings. Imagine yourself actively doing your hobby. Then, when you notice that small opening, stop the activity, get very small and dive into that opening.

Here is a dancing entrance. Imagine yourself dancing (but

don't put on dance music and listen to it). See yourself moving around the dance floor, and in your mindself, you can now hear any music you like. But don't dance for a long time or pay too much attention to whomever you are dancing with. Once you really see yourself on that dance floor, do a flip into the air. When you come down, imagine coming down so hard a crack appears in the dance floor and you just fall right into it, coming out... you guessed it, in the lower world.

How about just imagining being there? Remember I told you it took me a long time to start journeying? Well, this is the way I began my first real journey. I just daydreamed that I was there, in the lower world. I daydreamed that I was in a forest running down a path. I skipped everything I told you about how to get there. Why was this time different for me? What made this my first real journey? After months of trying the classic way, and expecting it to happen without using my imagination (without daydreaming), all the things my teacher, Aimee Morgana, had told me about finding my own way of journeying as opposed to only trying the ways I read about, finally shattered my stubbornness. I used my imagination, I made it up, and I daydreamed it. This is something you don't read about very often in shamanic books. I allowed myself to daydream. I gave myself permission to pretend, to use my imagination. Now, I give you permission to do the same. The most important thing was that when I found myself in the lower world, when I imagined myself in that forest, I believed I was there. I cannot stress the importance of that. Belief and trust are the most important aspects of a shamanic practice.

It was only after I was very comfortable journeying that I found that the easiest and quickest way for me to start a journey was to imagine a real tree that was in a park near my home. That tree had a huge hole in one side of its trunk and I always started my journeys by imagining that I was standing in front of that hole and I just jumped into that. That was my doorway for many years.

You can do the same thing I did. Daydream yourself in a place of nature, see it, imagine it, feel it, touch the ground, smell the air, hear the sounds around you. Believe you are there and you are.

Didn't like any of the ways you read? Then think of another way, your way. I told you how you enter spirit's world is not important. All that matters is that you allow your mindself to know it is leaving our reality and entering the spirit reality. Now, what are you going to do once you get there?

You are going to look for an animal guide. Call out. I don't mean speak in our reality. There are no sounds coming from your bodyself back in your room. Call out with your mindself. What could you say? How about, "I'm looking for my guide. Please come to me." That's it. Now, in your daydream, turn around, start walking, look to the sky or look to the ground. Usually, your guide will be there. But sometimes, you have to work for it. Don't see your guide right away? Ask for help. Ask anything you see or sense in your environment. Ask a rock, a tree, or a blade of grass. Ask the wind or clouds above. Remember, you are in the spirit world. Everything there has a voice. But usually, nothing will speak to you until you ask.

And how will they (and your guide) answer? If you expect to hear a foreign voice inside your head, don't. Not going to happen. Answer this question silently – how much is 3 times 3? Nine, correct? You heard the nine inside your head, in your own voice. That is how you will hear spirit's answers. And that is one of the main problems for beginning shamanic practitioners. Since you will hear spirit's answer in your own voice, you will say to yourself, "I am making this up. I'm talking to myself. It's not real."

I told you. You have to believe. You have to trust. Once you start getting information you know is true for you, it will be easier to believe and trust. But in the beginning, it may be difficult. So if you find it hard to believe in yourself, then believe in me.

If you can't find your guide, whatever you ask will answer, and do what the answer tells you. But don't worry. Most of the time your guide will be there. I told you, this will be your guide and she or he has been waiting most of your life for you to appear in their world.

Since this is your first journey, let's keep it simple. When you see your guide, ask the following questions.

1. Why are you my guide?
2. What are some of the lessons you wish me to learn?
3. What is happening in my life now that needs your help?
4. What is one thing I can do in my world that will help me now?

In future journeys, when you ask a guide for help on any issue concerning your life, it is important for you to ask this last question. Always say to your guide: What is the first step (action) that I can take in MY reality to bring what I have just learned into my life?

These are the questions I would like you to ask. But since this is your first meeting with your guide, you may have questions of your own. Ask them. Spirit guides come and go for reasons we don't understand. But there is a good chance this guide will be with you for a long time and it is important that you establish a good trusting relationship with her/him. Stay with your guide for as long as you wish, being there, talking, playing or dancing. Do whatever you need to do to lay the foundation of a solid relationship. And when you are ready, thank your guide for coming. Always thank your guides. Then, if you can, retrace your steps in getting to the spirit world. If you used the elevator, just imagine it behind you, turn and enter. If you used the cave, go back to it and walk home. If you forgot or find it difficult, or if you just daydreamed yourself there, begin to concentrate on your bodyself. Allow your mindself some time to adjust becoming one with the bodyself. Take a few deep breaths, open your eyes when you are ready, and you're back in your own room, in your own world. However, do not operate any heavy machinery, cars, trucks, snow blowers, chain saws or farming equipment, etc. until you are fully back in your own world.

There is one other thing I am going to suggest because most shamanic practitioners do it. (And I am sorry for asking this because you may not like it.) In a notebook, write down every-thing you can remember. Journeys, even though they are just like daydreams, have a night dream quality to them. You may forget many of the things you experienced in them. In a week, you will hardly remember anything. By writing them down, you will always be able to go back to your notebook and reread your notes.

PLEASE, STOP READING UNTIL YOU HAVE COMPLETED YOUR FIRST JOURNEY.

You started. You took your first journey. I hope it went well and you met your animal guide. It's impossible for me to know if it was difficult for you or if you weren't successful. But I would be a terrible teacher if I didn't assume that some of you saw only darkness no matter how hard you imagined. Unfortunately, all I can do to help is tell you some of the reasons I had problems along with some of the problems I think you might have experi-enced. If you had any of these, maybe what I say will help you overcome them. But don't give up. Remember, it took me several months and many attempts before I began journeying. It was a very frustrating few months.

You felt silly or even embarrassed being in a darkened room trying to contact spirits.

Every time your mindself drifted, you pulled it back because you knew it was just you, imagining something.

You said to yourself, if I am using my imagination, if I am

only daydreaming, none of this is real. This is dumb.

You didn't believe that mysterious indigenous shamans do something so simple as imagining a guide.

While on your journey, you spoke to something that answered in your voice, just like I said. You knew you made that up and opened your eyes.

Nothing happened. You tried your hardest for your daydream to start and it never did. You wanted it to be real, and for you, real meant it had to happen without you starting it. You would not daydream; it had to happen on its own.

Whatever obstacles stopped you from journeying, unless it was your cat who pounced on your chest, a phone call from the phone you didn't shut off, or a parent or sibling yelling, "What are you doing in there!" the answer to most common problems are the same. They are:

- You did not believe in yourself.
- You did not believe that you could imagine sending your mindself on a daydream and meeting a real spirit guide.
- You were so skeptical about the outcome, as soon as you started your expectations dropped to zero. You met your expectations. You knew nothing would happen so nothing did.
- You didn't trust me or believe in me when I said it would be really easy. You also didn't trust yourself.

As you read my answers to your problems, if you said, "Ah-ha" only once, please try the journey again. This time, TRUST in yourself. BELIEVE in yourself. Your guide has been waiting for you for a long time. Don't give up on her/him. When I gave you suggestions on how to begin your journey, I told you how, after months of trying unsuccessfully, I began my first real journey. The key was so simple that it eluded me for the longest time. I gave myself permission to daydream, to use my imagination.

When I did and I really believed in that daydream, that's when my shamanic career began. I'd like you to do the same.

There is a word – synchronicity. It means that sometimes, when two or more events happen that don't seem to be related, on a level that we may not understand, those events really are related. What does that mean? Things you think are just coincidence may not be. Events can be related even if we don't know what that relationship is. They may be happening for a reason that neither you nor I understand.

Let me give you a very silly but simple example. A car runs out of gas on your block. The driver drops his cell phone as he gets out of the car and it breaks. He walks to the nearest house, which happens to be yours. You are singing in the shower and the window is open. The driver hears you singing as he rings the bell to ask if he can use the phone to call the automobile club. The driver is a record producer and two months later your first record is released.

Those events don't seem to be related. But if the car hadn't run out of gas exactly where and when it did, if the cell phone hadn't fallen, if the person had chosen any other house, and if you weren't singing with the bathroom window open, you'd never have gotten that record contract.

That's synchronicity, and usually you can never tell what events are related (because not everything is) until you look back after the series of events have already happened.

How long have you been interested in shamanism? How did you learn about my book? Are there any events in your life happening right now that you might need help in dealing with? If you have been thinking about shamanism for a while, why decide to take action now, when you were in a position to learn about this book? Where were you when you learned about this book? Why were you there? How many events took place that led you to actually buying or downloading this book? Is it possible that if some of the answers to my questions did not occur, you might not be reading this book now? Is it possible that for some reason, either known to you or not, now is the time in your life that you need shamanism, you need a spirit guide, and you need someone who you can trust completely to help you in some way? (That would be your guide, not me.)

Some of the happenings in our lives do not occur in a vacuum. They happen for a reason (even if we never know what that reason is) and there is a reason you have turned to the shamanic path. If you had a problem in your first journey, please, attempt it again. You've all daydreamed, of that I am sure. Send out your mindself, tell it to give you the dream you are searching for. **Make it up.** Tell your mindself to make it up. It doesn't matter. It really doesn't. It will be real all the same.

IF YOU NEED TO REPEAT THE FIRST JOURNEY,
PLEASE DO IT NOW.

What You Need To Know About Spirit Guides

Spirit guides don't always give you answers that are easy to understand. Many times, it will seem that their answers make no sense to you. If that happens ask more questions.

Guides sometimes will not answer your questions. They never answer questions unless you are ready to hear the answers or they just may not want to. In either case, asking more questions may not help. But try anyway.

All guides are powerful. Power is not defined as physical strength. It's knowledge, it's wisdom. One of the questions I suggested you ask your animal guide was, "What are some of the lessons you wish me to learn?" Here's why that's important. A lioness can teach you about patience, an elephant can teach you how to use your own strengths most effectively, and a mole can teach you to see what you are missing about an issue in your life. Even in our world all animals have different attributes or character traits. Over a short distance, cheetahs are the fastest animals in the world. But they have to choose their prey wisely, for when they miss and their prey gets away, they have to wait a long time until they regain their strength before trying again. In the meantime, they go hungry. If a cheetah was your guide, what do you think she/he could teach you?

Time means nothing to spirit guides. Without going into lengthy explanations (that will come later), in shamanic terms, all time is equal. The past, the present, and the future are the same to your animal guides. Your guides can visit you any time during your life. She or he can take you back to your past or far into your future. So don't be surprised if when you go to your guide because of an immediate problem, she/he may not agree with the need for action at the moment. And later, I'll explain how going back into your past or ahead into your future can help you a great deal in your present.

Spirit has a sense of humor. Since they know so much, they tend not to take things seriously. They will tease you.

Your guides will know why you have come as soon as they see you. But you should still ask. If they don't let you, be firm. Ask your question anyway.

Spirit guides can take any shapes they wish. Supposing a snake appears and says she/he is your guide. Suppose you are really afraid of snakes, and you know you will not be able to deal with a snake, even if it is in the spirit world. Tell your guide how you feel and ask her/him to please change her/his shape until such a time that you will be comfortable seeing a snake as your guide.

Your guide wants to help you, and because of that, sometimes she/he will not answer your question nor will they even allow you to ask it, even if you insist. Instead of allowing you to journey on what you want, they will just whisk you away and show you something completely different. This is important because you need to know the following. Spirit will not give you what you WANT. Spirit will give you what you NEED. It sounds simple because we all think we know what is best for us. Truth is, sometimes we don't. We think that what we want is what we need. When spirit disagrees, spirit will always win. The matter is closed and arguing is a waste of time. When it happens to you, just go where your guide takes you.

The guide you have may not be with you forever. Spirit guides come and go. As you continue journeying, several other guides, as well as your main guide (the first one you found) may also appear. You may find that those other guides come when you need specific information or when your intention is to ask about a certain subject. There are reasons these other guides appear, but most of the time we'll never know what they are. You can ask, and if you're lucky, you'll get an answer.

After I began to journey, one such guide that appeared to me was Water Buffalo. I soon learned that he never answered any of my questions. As a matter of fact, when I asked anything of him, there was only silence inside my head. But he always took me someplace whether I asked to go or not. I soon realized that what Water Buffalo showed me was always more important than what I wanted to know, and after the first few times, I stopped asking him anything. I just followed him or jumped on his back and let him take me wherever he wanted.

Spirit guides know more about shamanism than I do and more than any teacher you may have in the future. Eventually, they will become your teachers. The wonderful thing about shamanism is once you become proficient in journeying, you may not need anyone. If you had no trouble taking your first journey (or completed it a second time), you are on your way to changing how to accept anything you read in this book. In your future, human teachers (including me) will become human guides. Our role will be that of advisors, just like your spirit guides. Only what you learn from them is more important than what you learn from us. If I tell you to journey on a certain topic, but spirit leads you in a different direction, forget what I told you. If instead of going down into the lower world you are pulled up towards the upper world, go with it. I believe you are perfectly safe when in spirit's care. Whenever there is a conflict between what I (or any future teacher) tell you to do and what spirit wants you to do, ALWAYS do what spirit says.

Journey 2

Traveling Within Your Journey

Start this journey the same way you did the last time and find your way to the lower world. However you reached it then, repeat the same process now. In the future, if you wish to try a different way, that's fine. Greet your guide when you meet and say anything you'd like. Remember, you want to have a relationship with your guide and this is only the second time you have met. Get to know each other. As soon as you have finished, state (tell) your guide the intent of this journey.

The main reason for going on a journey is called the intent. Sometimes, it can be as simple as wanting to hang out with your guide. But when you have a specific question or purpose, it is important to keep that intent, that reason, in your mindself as it goes out and looks for your guide. If your mindself begins to wander (and it will) and you start thinking about a homework assignment you haven't completed or anything else that is of this world, repeating the journey's intent over and over in your mindself should pull you back into your journey.

After you greet your guide and have stated your intent, in practically in every journey you take, your guides will go somewhere else. You must begin to learn different ways of following and this journey is as good a time as any to start. Your guide may fly away or jump into a lake and sink down and you had better be able to keep up. They may grab you and race into the distance, and before you know it, you will be in a completely different landscape. I think spirit was the real inventor of Star Trek's transporter. No matter what animal guide you have, they can all fly or walk through mountains, or do anything else they want that would be impossible to do in our reality. You will have to stay with them, and that is part of the fun of journeying. In case you are thinking of asking how can you follow them, let me answer before you ask. You, your mindself, are in the spirit world and you can do anything you imagine yourself doing. So, use that imagination. If your guide flies away, jump up and follow. If she/he just disappears and you see her/him on a distant mountain, just think about being there and you will be.

Intent of Journey 2

Say to your guide: Take me somewhere I need to go and show me something I need to know.

To repeat – go to the lower world and meet your guide. After you have said what you wish to say, tell your guide the intent. Then, let your guide take you wherever she/he wants you to go and really try to experience the journey. View what your guide shows you and question her/him if you are not sure why your guide has taken you to that place or if you don't understand anything that happened during your journey. Remember, you have specifically asked to see something you need to know. Your guide will have specific reasons for taking you on this journey but understanding those reasons is not a guarantee that is attached to this or any journey. If you don't understand something in a journey, ask your guide.

Will some of it be your imagination? Yes. Will some of it be outside your imagination? Yes. Will it matter which is which? No. It's all the same.

When you are satisfied that you have experienced enough, thank your guide and return to your bodyself that is waiting in your room. Again, either retrace your steps getting to the lower world or just return in that slow way I explained before, becoming aware of your bodyself and opening your eyes. (After I was comfortable journeying, this is the way I always returned to our reality.)

I hope that what you learn from this journey will have some relevance in your life. If so, it will be just a taste of what lies before you. If you begin to say, some of this is real, some of this is not all my imagination, that's great.

STOP READING UNTIL YOU HAVE COMPLETED YOUR JOURNEY.

If this were a workshop, we would now discuss what some of you saw, felt, experienced, and what you learned from the journey. Those of you who had issues would ask questions. Hopefully, those questions would be addressed in a way that helps solve them. But it's not a workshop and I have no idea what problems you might have faced. I'll try to give generic answers to questions you might have asked.

What if you didn't understand something, and even after questioning your guide, you were still in the dark? Here are 2 important things to remember when you ask your guide a question and don't get a satisfactory answer, which will happen many times. First, try NOT to ask a yes or no question. You take a journey to get information about something you need to know in your life now. Just hearing a yes or no doesn't really give you information. I know, sometimes you have to ask a yes or no question. If you do, follow it up immediately with a "Why." Second, if you don't get an answer you understand, try rephrasing the question or ask a related question that will give you a hint to what your guide is thinking. You ask, "I want to go to a concert and my parents said no. How can I get them to say yes?" But you don't get a satisfactory answer. Maybe try something like this, "What can I do in my real world to change my parents' minds?" or "My friends are going to the concert. What do I need to do (in my real world) to be able to go with them?" Slight differences in asking questions can sometimes make big differences in having them answered.

You, much more than I, live in an immediate world. When I was your age, there was no Internet. Oh, didn't I tell you I was that old? Sorry, I forgot. When I needed to communicate with someone, I used a rotary phone or wrote a letter. Those were my only choices. Today, on your smart phone, you can send a text message to a person who is 1000s of miles away and if that person is awake, you could get an answer immediately. If I wanted tickets to a concert, I had to go to the concert hall and buy them. Today, you can go online, many times even select your seats, put in a credit card number and print out your tickets. You expect immediate gratification and our world provides it. But spirit doesn't work that way. Time does not matter to the spirits you meet, and you will learn about that later in the book. Suppose in your journey you didn't get a full explanation, and after returning to our reality, you are confused about what you experienced. That's normal. Sometimes I think spirit's goal is to help us in the most confusing way they can. That's another reason why writing journeys in a Journey Journal is important. Even before doing the next journey in this book, you can journey back to your guide and ask questions specifically geared to the areas you are confused about. And by rereading your journal, you will be able to form your own intent.

I guess I forgot to tell you – being a shamanic practitioner is not always easy. Spirit makes you work for it.

However, I will try to help you as much as possible. To that end, I have an e-mail address, TeenShamanHelp@aol.com. If you're stuck and could use some advice, e-mail me. I'll do my best to do whatever I can to help you. You just have to be aware of the following. I could get anywhere from zero to 100s of e-mails. Therefore, when you e-mail, be as brief as possible. Don't tell me the story – just tell me the problem. If I need more information, I'll e-mail you. Also, my e-mail responses will depend on how many e-mails I have. By necessity, my answers will be brief. Finally, I use a Mac and sometimes AOL does weird things with my e-mails. But I'll check my spam folder, and hopefully, I will receive all e-mails.

Journey 3

Merge with Your Guide

There is a specific reason for the order of the journeys that I suggest you take. I have been a shamanic practitioner since 1995 and have done hundreds of journeys. I was a co-founder of the New York Shamanic Circle and that circle has become one of the most important shamanic communities in New York City. I have taught or assisted in many shamanic workshops. Llyn Roberts and I wrote a book on *Shamanic Reiki*. Dr. Eve Bruce and I wrote a book on shamanic journeying. My main teachers have been indigenous shamans from Brazil and Peru as well as many Western shamans. Though I prefer to call myself a shamanic practitioner, my indigenous teachers and members of the community I helped serve in NYC have called me shaman. But to be honest, since moving to Florida where there are no shamanic communities that I can find, the term shamanic practitioner suits me fine. (For Your Information –FYI– Shamans are named so by the community they serve. They should not name themselves.)

Once you feel comfortable on the shamanic path you have chosen to walk, you may need very little help in journeying. You can journey to your guide any time you wish and the intent of those future journeys can be anything you want. My goal is to lead you on journeys that will allow you to experience the many different aspects of the journey, and how you can navigate the spirit world. It is to introduce you to different types of guides and how by doing specific types of journeys can get you the kind of information you want in the easiest way possible.

By following the steps I am giving you, when you finish reading this book you should be able to accept whatever experience spirit presents you with. You ought to feel confident that no matter what the problem is, you will always have a friend and ally in spirit. Even though you are just beginning, within a short time you will be able to journey for any reason with the same confidence that shamanic practitioners like myself have when we journey.

Please remember that if you wish to repeat a journey for any reason, whether you change the intent a little to make it more personal to you, keep it the same, or change it completely, that's perfectly acceptable.

Earlier, I told you about your two selves, the bodyself and the mindself. Now, I'm going to tell you about two other selves you have. These selves are much more difficult to separate. One is the emotional self and the other is the intellectual self. I could spend pages in explaining the difference, but for now, I want to keep it simple. The obvious definitions are the following.

The emotional self is that part of you that is guided and controlled by your emotions. When you allow that self to lead your actions, you don't want to listen to logic. You don't want to listen to anything that anyone says that is contrary to what you want.

Best example would be a very young child, 4 or 5 years old. They want what they want when they want it. And if they don't get it immediately, watch out. You can't be as bad as that. If you want that last piece of cake in the refrigerator, and your mom say you're having dinner in ½ an hour and she's saving that for your dessert, you are not going to throw a tantrum.

They say never discuss two things in polite society: politics or religion. The reason is most adults have definite ideas about each of those topics and those ideas are deeply rooted in their belief systems. And most people are highly emotional when it comes to their belief systems. When we are very emotionally attached to something, we usually feel that everyone should have the same belief as ours. If they don't, then they are just plain wrong.

Your intellectual self is, of course, ruled by your intellect. It is ruled by logic. The intellectual self can be persuaded but emotional arguments may not work.

Here is an example of how the two may operate differently. Last year your family went to a hotel near the ocean and you really had a good time. You bring up the topic during dinner and suggest that you go back to the same place. Before you change your opinion about your vacation choice, you have to hear reasons that appeal to you; that make sense to you. If you get enough reasons, you may change your mind. Your dad may say, "We have a little extra money, so how about going to Disney World or maybe even visiting your aunt who lives in Europe!" Might you change your mind?

But suppose your current significant other's family is going to the same beach you went to last year at the same time your family is going on a vacation. What do you think? Would your emotional self or intellectual self dictate your behavior during the discussion? Your dad could say the same things but would they do any good?

Emotions aren't bad and play a major role in all of our lives. We just have to know which self is dictating our current behavior and that's very difficult even for adults. During a shamanic journey, emotions, how you feel, must rule. During journeys, the intellectual self is not your friend. It will tell you time and time again nothing is real because a shamanic journey cannot stand up to logic. You're making it up; you're playing pretend. You have to talk down that self. You have to tell your intellectual self to wait in your bodyself while you are taking a journey. You don't want it with you. You need to tell that self that you will be fine without it for a little while and you will meet up with it when you return.

An important aspect of any journey is how you feel, both during and after it. When a journey feels right, when you know whatever is happening is just what you need when you need it, then shamanism is working for you.

Journey 3 is purely to experience the emotions of being in the spirit world. Though you will find your guide, you don't have to ask her/him anything except stating the intent. I don't want you to use your intellect. That part of you will only tell you what you are going to do is not real so don't do it, or worse, don't believe the feelings you are going to experience.

Intent of Journey 3

Say to your guide: Will you allow me to merge with you? (I have never had a person tell me the guide refused.)

What does that mean? You are asking your guide to allow you to enter him or her and you do that by just stepping into the guide. You want to merge with your guide. You want to be 'one' with your guide. You want to see from her or his eyes. You want to experience how your guide moves, feels, and thinks. You want to taste the energy that comes from being one with your guide. In the spirit world, energy can sometimes be a tangible thing. You may be able to feel it with your mindself, and then your bodyself, waiting for you in your room, may also feel it. This idea of feeling energy will become very important later on. Since this is the first time you are merging with your guide and experiencing the journey, try to not only feel the energy coming from your guide, but also try to remember it. What does the energy feel like when you are part of your guide? Do you think you will be able to reproduce that energy in your bodyself when you are fully back in our world? If not, don't worry about it. If not now, later, I promise you.

And your guide doesn't have to be big and powerful like a bear, a wolf or an eagle for you to feel all the things I said. Your guide can be a dove, a rabbit or an otter. All guides are powerful, and whether it is the energy of a diving hawk or the gentle breeze created by a butterfly landing on a flower, try to experience the energetic power of being that animal guide.

You don't have to say anything to your guide except the intent in the beginning and the grateful thank you at the end. I want you to experience everything your guide does. You don't have to do anything in this journey other than being part of your guide. Oh, you can ask your guide anything you wish. This journey will begin to cement your relationship so say anything, ask anything that you feel needs to be said or asked while you are merged with your guide. Nothing can hurt you while you and your guide are one. Nothing can harm you. Just remember, you can't stay there forever and you have to come back to our world. How will you know when? Your guide will know, and at that same moment, so will you.

STOP READING UNTIL YOU HAVE COMPLETED YOUR JOURNEY.

How did it go? I hope you felt the wonder of the experience. You were completely yourself and completely in charge of you and did not lose control of your mindself. But at the same time you were you – you also weren't you. You were not WITH your guide; you WERE your guide. The sights, the sounds, and the smells were your guide's experiences. And yet, they were also your experiences, weren't they? I hope you really felt the power and energy of the journey, the power and energy of being part of your guide. Sounds a bit crazy, doesn't it. Don't worry. We're both sane. Well, at least I am.

FYI: If you ever do begin to feel uncomfortable during a journey and though you ask your guide, the flavor of the journey remains the same and you wish to end it immediately, just open your eyes. Later, after you have thought about why you were uncomfortable, do another journey with the intent of telling your guide you were uncomfortable and asking her/him why you were uncomfortable and what you should do if something similar occurs in the future.

Journey 4

Find an Ancestor

Remember I told you about Water Buffalo and how, whenever he showed up, I knew that asking questions was useless and I just needed to go along? All guides have different personality traits and the more you work with them, the more obvious those traits become. When you are a little more experienced in journeying, which won't take long, you'll learn to recognize the difference between your guides. You may want to journey to specific guides because you know that it may be easier to get the answers for your questions from them or that they are the best source to get the information you are looking for.

Shamanic practitioners often journey to ancestors. Let me define that term. If I ask you to name an ancestor, you might try to remember the name of your great-grandfather or some other relative from your past. Yes, those ancestors are available to you in a journey. But the word means much more. It can also mean someone or something that has a great deal of knowledge and/or wisdom. One of the ancestors I journeyed to was a tree, a very old ancient tree. I asked the tree permission to become one with it, to merge with it, and then I entered the trunk. Almost immediately I felt the weight of extreme age and the calmness that comes with that age. And when my mindself spoke to him, the ancestor answered.

There is no telling who or what your guide will take you to when you ask to be taken to an ancestor. Your guide could drop you in front of a small house by a stream, on a mountain, in the middle of a desert or in a forest. It might be a person, but also it might not.

I just said that your personal ancestors are also there, ready to help and counsel you. They can be a good source of information for you because you may have already spent part of your life building up a relationship with that person while the person was alive. The trust you need to have in a guide is already there.

This is my example of how my parents became part of my ancestor guides. My father died in 2002 after being married to my mother for over 60 years. The last few years were not easy for her because my father was suffering from dementia. His mind was not right. My mom never got over his death and spent the last eight years of her life just waiting for hers to end. She was over 100 years old when she passed so I had no regrets over her death. I was with her at the end and it was a long night. At one point, I sensed my father was in the room and knew my mother's time was short. Was he really there, in that room, in our reality? No. Was he there in the shamanic reality? Yes. Because of the years I had spent being a practitioner, when I felt his presence, I never doubted it for a moment. Did I imagine him standing in the doorway of the bedroom? Yes. Did it matter? No.

Several weeks after she passed, I journeyed to her. My intent was just to say a final goodbye and to tell her everything in my life would be fine. I saw both my parents when they were young. I guessed in their early 30's, around the time they were married. They were walking, holding hands, on a sidewalk. I don't know where they were and it didn't matter. They were smiling and very happy. I knew that their happiness came from being together again. Just like I will tell you later, I started talking to them, telling them who I was. I must have found them at a time before I was born because I felt they didn't recognize me. They didn't even turn to me or acknowledge me. So I left, feeling very warm and toasty knowing they were happy and content being together. Later, I journeyed back to them, but I asked my guide to take me to a time when they would know who I was. They did and it was a rewarding journey. And from then on, both of my parents became part of my ancestor guides.

FYI: I told you that journeys are about feelings. In my example, when I first went to find my mother, the power of the journey was in the way I felt about what I experienced. Yes, the spirits of my parents did not talk to me. But since I felt that was just the way it was supposed to be, I was fine with it. I knew I could come back and things might be different. I did and they were. Trust your feelings. During your journeys, they are very important. Try not to have expectations when you journey. Events will occur that you would not have thought about if you could plan out beforehand what will happen during your journey. When those unexpected events occur during a journey, don't analyze, don't involve your intellectual self. If it feels right, accept it and move forward from there, even if it means changing your intent. If it doesn't feel right, ask questions until it does.

I said ancestors do not have to be related to you. In your journey, you are going to ask your guide to take you to an ancestor. Do not say MY ancestor but AN ancestor. If you say "my" it may imply that you wish an ancestor related to you. That restricts your guide. If you say "an" you allow your guide to pick the ancestor you need at that moment in your life. Different ancestors have different knowledge and the one your guide will take you to will be the one you need the most, even if you don't think you need an extra dash of wisdom in your life.

Remember, though ancestors usually are in human form, they don't have to be. If you have a problem understanding who or what your ancestor is, ask your guide. If you have a problem communicating with the ancestor, ask your guide.

When you reach the ancestor, ask what advice she/he can give you regarding a situation you are having in your life now. It doesn't have to be a major problem either. Since this is the first time you are visiting an ancestor select an easy problem.

Don't forget to thank the ancestor before you leave, and I

always included in my goodbye the question, "May I come again?" The answer, based on my experience, is always yes. Guides are there to help us, remember? But it is polite to ask anyway.

Intent of Journey 4

Ask your guide to take you to an ancestor. Ask the ancestor what advice she/he can give you regarding a problem you are having in your life now.

STOP READING UNTIL YOU HAVE COMPLETED YOUR JOURNEY.

If you take this journey several times, you may find that each time you do, your guide takes you to a different ancestor, depending on the problem. If you want to visit a specific ancestor, you should include that in your intent of your future journeys.

Yet, even as I wrote that last sentence, I am not sure I want you to actually do it. One of life's inconveniences is every so often we get sick and have to go to a doctor. Usually, you go to the family doctor but, sometimes, you go to a specialist, a doctor who only deals in one area, an area of their expertise. Comparing your guide to your family doctor is an analogy I hope you can understand. When you ask your guide for something, just as your family physician knows if she/he can solve your problem or if you need a specialist, so does your guide. By confining your intent and asking for a specific ancestor, you negate the possibility that a different ancestor might be able to be a better advisor for your particular problem. Does it really matter? No. All spirit guides will give you information if you ask. But would it be easier to go to a guide who specializes in the kind of information you are seeking? Yes. I would always trust your guide... well, most of the time. But if you believe very strongly in visiting a certain ancestor, tell your guide. Insist on it.

Also, this will be the last time I ask you to stop reading and journey before continuing. You will have done 4 journeys and should feel confident enough to know you CAN do this any time you wish. As you read, you may find a journey that is exactly what you need in your life now. If you hesitate doing journeys out of order, don't e-mail to ask permission. You have it. With each journey you complete, my role as a teacher diminishes and your guide's role rises. Ask your guide.

> FYI: What did the experience feel like? Did you experience a difference between your guide and the ancestor? Did the ancestor seem to know anything about you? Did the ancestor give you any advice that you thought either was or could be helpful? Do you think you may be able to apply that advice to the specific problem, or can you generalize it and place it in the category of things you should remember? When you questioned the ancestor, were you satisfied with the answers? If not, did you continue questioning? If not, why? If you are not content with what these questions may have brought up, I suggest you return to the source and journey back to your guide with the intent of finding out the answers.

Journey 5

Detaching Yourself

In Journey 3, I briefly discussed the difference between your emotional self and your intellectual self. We're going to go a little deeper into that now. As a matter of fact, we are going to begin to go into what I call heavy or difficult journeys. By difficult I don't mean that the procedure, how you begin the journey, will change. It's the same; it's always the same. Difficult journeys are hard because of the nature of their intents. In this journey, you will ask your guide to show you a part of yourself that you might not wish to look at very closely. You may discover things about yourself in ways you may not have thought about. The word for that is introspection, and that means taking a good hard look at you. But one of the reasons for becoming a shamanic practitioner is to understand yourself better, to be able to cope more fully with whatever life is presenting you with, and you can't do that without looking deeply into yourself.

Detachment means separation, and that means keeping things apart. This journey is to show you how to begin to separate the things within you that need to be kept apart.

Beginning in 2010 and continuing at least into mid-2013 (the time this book was written), the United States Congress was almost completely inefficient. In my opinion, one of the only things they did together was deposit their paychecks into the bank. Why were they so terrible? Why were the American people so disgusted with their politicians? Again, my opinion is those politicians could not separate their emotional selves from their intellectual selves.

I have just used the word opinion twice. You know the difference between fact and opinion? A fact can be proven. A fact is true for everyone. The sun rises every morning and sets every evening. That's a fact. Watching a sunrise, especially on a beach, is beautiful. That's an opinion. Two people watching the same sunrise in the same place at the same time can each have a different opinion. One can love it but the other may think the sight was not worth getting up so early for. However, they are both correct. Opinions are personal. Neither person can deny that the sun rose because facts are true for everyone. If what is true for me is not true for you, then that's an opinion. But let me get back to the US Congress.

Everyone agreed that the US government was spending much more money than it had and that meant it had to borrow trillions of dollars to pay the country's bills. That was a fact. However, how to stop it, how to pay for what was already spent and come up with a budget that would allow the government to be able to pay for what they will spend in the future without borrowing was not easy because that falls under the realm of opinion. I believe (an opinion word) that the politicians in both parties didn't think their solutions were opinions. They believed them to be facts. Some said raise taxes to collect more money. Some said spend less by stopping programs the government was paying for or giving those programs much less money. And some said, let's try to compromise.

Which group do you think was ruled by their intellectual selves? I think the last. They realized that by compromising no one would get exactly what they wanted. But everyone could get some of what they wanted. The problem was that this third group had the least amount of politicians and could not effect a change by themselves.

Most of the elected officials were so rigid in their beliefs that they refused to compromise because (and again, this is my opinion) they were so emotionally attached to their opinions that they believed that their opinions WERE facts. Since facts are true for everyone, that meant anyone who didn't believe as they did was just wrong. And why listen, why compromise with people if they are wrong?

Now, what does all this have to do with you? Each one of us, and I include myself, are like the politicians I just described. We all have beliefs that govern our behavior. Many of the beliefs that we treat as truths are, in reality, opinions. Now there is absolutely nothing wrong with that. Opinions shape us into who we are; into the kind of people we want to become. But sometimes it is important to separate a fact from an opinion in our belief system. We can still have the same belief; we just have to realize that the belief is not a universal fact. We must accept that others may have opposing ideas about 'our facts' and doing so does not make them wrong. By accepting this, we acknowledge that there is room within our belief to allow others to have different opinions. There is an old cliché: "Live and let live." For me, it means as long as it does no harm, allow me to believe and act on my beliefs and I will allow you to believe and act on your beliefs.

The example I gave earlier was about a family vacation and a significant other. But that was an obvious one. I want you to think of any argument you recently had where both you and the other person ended up being annoyed at each other because each of you maintained that you were correct. Now that you are not emotionally involved in the argument, think about it. Being honest, was your point a fact? Was what you wished true for everyone, even me? If not, then it was an opinion. And remember, you don't change a person's mind with your emotional attachments. You change it with logic. Neither of you accepted that you each had an opinion, and you were both being ruled by your emotional selves. Neither of you realized that both of you were correct. And the only way to solve both being correct was for both of you to compromise. This journey is NOT to change your mind about that argument, but to open your mind up to the possibilities that lie in your future if you can detach yourself from fact Vs. opinion.

You're going to journey to your guide. As in the past, you are going to state your intention and I suggest you let the guide decide how best to answer your question.

Intent of Journey 5

Ask your guide: Show me why a belief I have that I think is a fact is really an opinion. What do I need to know so I can separate my facts from my opinions in the future, and how can I begin to do that in my life?

This may not be an easy journey because it may force you to look deeply into yourself. You may find something that is or will be important for you to know now or in the future. Changing your mind about any issue or belief you have at this point is not important. What is essential is that you begin to learn that being a citizen of your family, school, community, city or world is more than I want what I want when I want it. It is being able to recognize that what you want may not be what others want, and other people's opinions are just as valid to them as yours are to you. Both of you can be correct, and both of your answers are of equal importance. That means that even though you may not accept the opposing opinion, you should at least respect it and allow the other person to have her/his opinion without getting into a shouting match.

FYI: Now that you are aware of how believing your opinion is a fact affects you, I'd like you to think about other instances in your past when understanding the difference might have affected the outcome. Think about what you could have said or could have done that would have resolved a problem better than it was resolved in reality.

Journey 6

Dismemberments

Again, a difficult journey for you to accomplish at this early stage of your shamanic career. But you might as well do it now because if you don't do it with me, you'll do it with your guide when you least expect it. All the people in my shamanic circle, all the people I have worked with in the past have had dismemberment journeys to one degree or another. Many times, the first dismemberment journey is not asked for but just happens when their guides decide it's time.

What is dismemberment? The word means removing a limb from your body or dividing something up or destroying something by taking it apart. Guess what, in a dismemberment journey, you ARE that something! And that's what you are going to ask your guide to do to you in this journey.

I just said that most of the people I knew in my shamanic circle or that I spoke to in the workshops I taught or assisted with have experienced a dismemberment journey on their own, without being instructed to do so. With the same belief I have that shamanism is real, I believe that spirit, who gives us what we need when we need it, will take you (or only a part of you) apart whenever it wants to, regardless how you will feel about it. It's just easier if you do it before spirit surprises you. Then you will know what to expect when spirit does it on its own.

So what's the journey? I want you to ask your guide to perform a dismemberment journey on you. Tell your guide to fix whatever part of you needs fixing the most and put it back together in a way that helps you the most. This way, you are leaving it up to your guide.

My first time was also an unasked for journey. My guide took me over a volcano and he plunged into the molten lava, I just

40

followed. I told you, you have to keep up with your guide, didn't I? I remember melting until I was just bones. The bones didn't melt and I kept going down, deeper into the lava, following my guide. Soon, we came out under the water. I moved up until I reached the surface and floated to a beach. I walked up the sand and lay down. Then my guide poured sand over me and blew into my head. That's when I felt myself become whole again.

I didn't ask for that first journey but I went with the experience. I felt as much as I could, the heat, the melting – the being in a state of just floating and feeling the rawness within me. When my guide finished reassembling me, I felt the newness of being whole again. It was the first time in a long time that I remembered feeling so complete. I didn't ask questions. I just went with the experience. That was an error and I fixed that the next time I went back and asked for a dismemberment journey. But you are expecting that kind of journey and I want you to ask the question I should have asked.

Intent of Journey 6

Say to your guide: Take me on a dismemberment journey. Fix whatever part of me needs it most and put it back together in a way that helps me the most.

During or after the journey, when it feels right, ask the following. (I suggest that instead of asking these questions during the journey, you just experience it first and then ask. The reason is that after experiencing the whole journey, you may find that you already know the answers to some of the questions.)

- What did you do?
- Why did you take (name the part) apart?
- What was wrong with the part or parts you took?
- What did you do to fix what you removed?
- How will the new part help me more than the old?

- And a most important question, how can I bring the changes you made in me into my life now?

Don't worry. Your guide will always put you back together. Well, most of the time they do.

I told you spirit will give you what you need and not what you want, and it will not answer questions unless you are ready. If you have difficulties with this journey, or if something else occurs, go with the something else. I don't remember how long I was practicing shamanism when spirit took me on my first dismemberment journey. I'm pushing the envelope with you by asking you to do this journey now, after only 5 previous journeys. Neither you nor I will know when you are ready. If you can't achieve this journey now, don't worry. You will be able to do it later. Just don't forget to do it later. Spirit won't.

FYI: When, in the future, spirit just does a dismemberment journey on its own when your intention is to do something else, try to remember the questions you asked in this journey and sneak them in after the journey is over. I want you to think about the following: what did it FEEL like as the guide removed the part or parts of you? What did it FEEL like as the guide was fixing the part? What did it FEEL like after you were put back together? Remember those feelings, and when we discuss bringing 'feelings' back from a journey, I want you to bring that last feeling back to your bodyself. It's important to learn that feeling, for it is the feeling of being healed!

Before we move on to the next journey, I want to say this. If you have done all the journeys and have received information that I hope you found relevant in your current situations, then you should be very happy with yourself. You have satisfied your curiosity about shamanism. You have tasted 6 different types of journeys, and you know that each one holds many possibilities because you can repeat them as often as you wish. Each time you do it's just like taking the journey for the first time. You are beginning to learn about spirit's reality. You are beginning to feel comfortable as you travel from place to place, and you have worked with different spirit guides. You have done far more than I when I began. But the most important thing you have accomplished is you are able to allow your mindself to travel to the spirit world and hopefully you said to yourself, "Is this real or is this my imagination?" fewer and fewer times after each journey. If not now, soon you will leave your intellectual self behind and allow your mindself free rein in the other world.

Journey 7

Find Your Guide in the Upper World

You just completed a few difficult journeys and deserve a break, an easy one. The journeys I have asked (and will ask) you to take are going to make a difference in your life, if you let them. They will also give you a more detailed view of the spirit world. You are learning, by experience, the boundaries of that other reality and how to go about accomplishing what you wish when you are on your own. This journey will continue that knowledge. It will be just like the first one you took and has the same intent. The only difference is you are going to go to the upper world.

Getting there is just as easy as getting to the lower world. The obvious difference is that instead of starting your journey by going down, start it by going up. I could say that if you have trouble reaching it, go on an up escalator and keep going or take the elevator and push the UW button instead of the LW one. But I won't. Just go up. Imagine yourself just rising up, through the ceiling of your room and the other apartments above you if there are apartments above you. When you reach the open sky, keep going. Eventually, many practitioners notice a white fog above them and enter it. That's the boundary between the middle world and the upper one.

Now some people break through the boundary and they are there. I didn't. I won't describe (except in very general terms) what I imagined because our journeys are unique to us. What you experience in your journey is your experience, and how spirit presents itself to you and what it means are both special to you. Never let anyone tell you what your journey or the objects you may encounter in your journey may mean. However, if they say before they give you their opinion, "If your journey were my journey, it would mean this to me," then listen and see if it makes any sense to you. If what you are told has some relevance to you, then you can use that as the basis for trying to decipher the meaning. I hope you understand the difference between the two ways of telling you.

But to continue, most of my journeys were not to the upper world. When I went (or when I was pulled up, as will happen) I saw the fog that I described. As I sensed myself continuing to move higher, the fog thickened beneath me but thinned in front of me. At some point, I imagined that the air was clear and I could see in the distance. When I looked down, I saw the fog that I was standing on had become solid. Most of the time, I knew when the journey was over because the fog lost its solidity and I just began to float down.

> FYI: Whenever I journeyed to the upper world, I encountered the fog. Will you encounter the fog? I don't know. Does it make a difference? No. But when I journeyed beyond our world to the Spirit of the Moon, for example, I never saw the fog. This reinforced for me the idea that Spirit, that all encompassing force that is filled with love, understanding, and compassion for all of us, is there, is real, and wants to help us.

When you have reached the upper world, call out and ask for a guide to come to you. Usually, that guide will be in human form, but not always. I think in shamanism there are very few of 'this will never happen' or 'this will always happen'. But there are lots and lots of this will usually happen. If you have trouble finding a guide, from within the journey, call out and ask your animal guide to come up and meet you. When that guide appears, ask her/him to take you to your upper world spirit guide.

Intent of Journey 7

Find your guide in the upper world. Ask:

1. Why are you my guide?
2. What are some of the lessons you wish me to learn?
3. What is happening in my life now that needs your help?
4. What is one thing I can do in my world that will help me now?
5. How are you different from my other guide (or guides)? The answer to this may not be direct. It may be more in the vein of, "You will have to discover the answer to this question yourself."

I found that my upper world guide tended to be more mysterious than my lower world ones. Maybe that was why I didn't go there that often. Many times when the journey ended I had only a vague idea what the journey meant and had to journey to my regular guides for clarification.

You may also ask any other questions in addition to mine or, if you feel your questions are more important than mine, ask yours instead. You could also say, "Who are you?" but don't expect an answer.

When you finish, thank the guide and return to our world by sinking back into the middle world.

Journey 8

Enter the Void

This may or may not be a difficult journey. The reason for this is I'm not going to give you the intent. You aren't going to know what this journey is about until you are in the journey. You are not going to know what's supposed to happen until it does.

I'm going to ask you to enter the void. Now you know the word void means vacant, empty space, nothing. How, you may ask, can you journey into nothing? The easiest way to tell you about this journey is to explain what I did when I discovered the void. Then I'll ask you to do the same.

I told you, in the beginning, I just imagined myself in the spirit world. After I began to trust my imagination, I did it the easier way – I imagined the real tree I told you about in the park near my house, the one with the large hole in it. I just saw myself jump into the hole and almost immediately came out in a cave. I always appeared in the back and could see the entrance before me. To one side, there was a large boulder standing away from the walls. This was where I met Raccoon, my first guide. He was with me for several years and he became a trusted friend. Usually Raccoon was waiting for me, sitting on the top of the boulder. I soon learned that if he was there, we would leave the cave together and the adventure of the journey would begin.

When he was not there, something different always happened. Those happenings always reinforced for my mindself and my intellectual self (who, in the beginning, always seemed to tag along) that the journey was real and not just imagined. What I just said is very important and you need to remember it, assuming you haven't figured it out for yourself. Sometimes, something in your journey will happen that is so out of the ordinary that you know you could never imagine it. A simple example would be if your journey took you to a tropical beach, and while walking on the sand, you saw an igloo surrounded by snow and a few Alaskan huskies. Aside from spirit's saying you need to find out who or what is inside the igloo, it should reinforce for both your mindself and intellectual self that shamanism works, the spirit reality is real and you are a traveler that can enter it whenever you wish.

But let's get back to how I discovered the void. I told you that sometimes Raccoon was not in the cave. Before going outside to search for him, I always looked around the cave. During one such journey when Raccoon wasn't there, I saw something new, a hole in the ground on the far side of the boulder. Since it wasn't there before, I knew it was placed there for me. So after a bit of hesitation, or maybe a lot, I jumped into it.

> FYI: You are beginning to create for yourself a map of your spirit world. Six times I have asked you to go to your main guide. By now, you should know the terrain, the landscape where you meet your guide. Pay attention each time you meet your guide there. If you notice something different, that difference is probably for you. Explore it, with or without your guide.

It wasn't very often, but each time I saw that hole, I knew what I had to do, jump in. That hole was what I call The Void. Your void may be completely different. You'll find out in a little while. I always fell into complete blackness. I couldn't see or sense anything except falling. And the longer I fell, the faster I felt I was falling. Eventually I realized that I had to slow down. I tried different things to do that. I imagined myself holding balloons or Mary Poppins' umbrella. Sometimes I looked down into the blackness below and blew air out of my mouth. As long as I could imagine it, it worked and I eventually slowed. When I finally reached the bottom, there was always enough light to see. And I always saw a door. I opened the door and entered. Then the real journey began. The void was my entrance to something spirit wanted me to know.

What I experienced each time I entered the door makes no difference because they were my void journeys. But each journey was completely different. You will experience your void journey in your own way and find out what spirit has planned for you. There is nothing I can tell you about what to expect. However, in my experience, none of my void journeys were terrifying or even scary, and many times they gave me information about something that I may not have thought of as being important enough to journey on. But spirit had a different idea. And usually spirit will win out in any discussion about what's important or not.

Just as most practitioners have or will have a dismemberment journey, they also have a void journey. Sometimes, especially if it happens when you aren't expecting it, entering a deep blackness can be scary. Sometimes it isn't. But if you do one now, then when it occurs on its own you'll have an idea of what to expect.

I want you to journey to your guide and ask her/him to take you to the entrance to your void. Then I want you to enter your void and see what happens. You may ask your guide to come with you, but that may or may not happen. Raccoon never came with me. He was never there when I entered. I hope that the entrance to your void is near your meeting place. That way, whenever you journey, regardless of the intent, if spirit wishes you to enter the void, you will see or sense it near you. If that happens, lose your planned intent and do what you have to. If your guide takes you to a void entrance that is not near your meeting point, please look around; search that area carefully so you will recognize it the next time you are taken there. If, in the future, you journey to the spirit world and instead of appearing in your regular meeting place you find that you are in this location, the void will be waiting for you. I suggest you always see what it holds.

By asking your guide to do this for you, you become familiar with a journey that you will have to take eventually. You might as well take it on your terms.

Intent of Journey 8

Say to your guide: Take me to the entrance of my void. Then enter and experience what spirit has in store for you.

As I said, don't expect what I envisioned. It probably won't happen that way. Also, the knowledge you receive the first time may not be connected in any way to the knowledge you will receive the second time. That's what makes the void special. Each time you enter, you open yourself up to a true spiritual experience. Having no idea what is coming, having no preplanned notions that your intellectual self can plant in your mindself, you open yourself up to the possibilities that what spirit is telling you is important for you to know, either now or in your future. As an additional bonus, the unexpected void always reinforces the idea that this isn't all your imagination.

FYI: I began keeping my journey journals in late 1995 and kept writing them for the first 5 or 6 years. I even input them into my computer because I have a really bad handwriting. Honestly, I didn't do it all the time because I tended to be lazy (still am to a larger degree than I'd like to admit) but I made sure I entered all the journeys when I didn't understand many parts of them, even after asking my guide questions. Sometimes, I was able to understand spirit's message to me when I reread my journal in the future. Many times, the knowledge I received in a current journey gave me a clue to understanding a past one. Being able to read about those past journeys was always important. I remember it took me a long time to find the past journey I needed because in the beginning I forgot to write the date and the intents of my journeys at the top of each entry. I had to skim over lots of journeys to find the one I wanted. I say this because if you are writing a journal, I suggest you begin each entry by writing the date and the intention. If you don't wish to go back and add these now, start doing it with the next journey. And, if there was something scary or uncomfortable in this journey, recall the specific occurrence. Then ask yourself, why did it make you frightened or uncomfortable? What in your past birthed that fright, and if it is important enough, journey to your guide and ask how you can begin to rid yourself of that fear.

Lessons Learned 1

You know how to reach your guide and question her/him about whatever is important to you. I told you once time does not matter and you will find that out in Journey 10. You may ask your guide about anything that has happened in the past, that is happening now, or that may happen in the future.

You have felt the energy and power of the spirit world when you merged with your animal guide. You can feel that same spirit power by merging with anything else in the spirit world as long as you ask and receive permission. You can merge with and be part of a mountain, you can feel its energy and know its wisdom if you think that the qualities of a mountain will help you in your current situation. You can experience being anything that dwells in the spirit world, if you want. And as I told you, if you were not able to recall the energy of your guide and bring it back with you into our world, you soon will.

You have met an ancestor and hopefully understand the difference between asking the ancestor or your guide for help. You should begin to realize that different guides might give you different information. When you know that you really need to understand an issue before you can solve it, going to an ancestor is not a bad idea.

You realized that the opinions you hold shape your attitudes and behavior. You have begun to understand that by using shamanic techniques, you can look at yourself in a different light, a light that can help you to become the person you wish to be. This does not mean you have to change who you are. But it should help you understand who you are better.

In the dismemberment journey, you have seen just a part of how spirit views you, and if that view is different from the way you see yourself. You may not have agreed with why spirit fixed the part of you it did. What you do with that information is up to you. But the fact that you are aware of it means you have begun to think about yourself in a different way. Knowing how and why spirit fixed a part of you might give you clues for either future journeys, or, if you agreed with spirit, you may even consider what you could do to help those changes take place in our reality.

You have begun to explore the upper world, and like the ancestor, have begun to discover the difference between the upper world guide and the lower world guide. One journey to each is by far not enough, but it is a beginning.

In entering the void, you learned to pay attention to your surroundings in the spirit world and be aware that changes in scenery that you are familiar with are important. You have learned that spirit knows you better than you think. In the void journey, without asking, I hope you found relevance. You also should have received additional validation that shamanism works. It's real.

Remember, shamanism is about you and how you can become the person you really want to be. I wonder if you thought you were just having fun and playing pretend? Well, you weren't.

Journey 9.0

Energy Vampires, Part 1

This journey is important because what you learn from it can be used in this world, in this reality, as many times as you need it. Though it specifically targets energy vampires, the techniques to protect yourself from them can be applied in any situation your imagination thinks those techniques will help.

If you Google Energy Vampire, you will find that many of the articles you read speak about people who drain your energy by their actions. Those people are the ones who are constantly negative about everything, constantly complaining, and constantly trying to drag you into their story. They are the naysayers, the blamers, the gossipers and the drama queens. They are the people who think that everything that happens should revolve around them, and expect or demand that everyone recognize their importance in the total scheme of the Universe. Yes, these people drain your energy. But I'm not referring to them because you know who these energy vampires are; and avoiding them, if you can, is your best defense.

It might be easier to know the people I mean if I used the words psychic vampires instead. These people drain your energy without your knowledge. These are the people you need to protect yourself from the most. You won't be alone in doing this because spirit is more than willing to help protect you, even when you may not realize you need protection.

Have you ever walked into a room when you are feeling fine and soon found yourself sad or tired or angry (or another emotion) for no reason? Have you ever felt energy around you without knowing where it is coming from, but your instinct tells you that the energy is no good for you? Usually, but not always, it may occur when you enter a room or crowded space for the first time. If you are really happy, did you ever notice that when you feel that way, others around you just perk up? Whether you knew it or not, you were sending out your energy and other people were picking that up. Did you ever walk into a classroom before a test, and though you were confident because you studied, you suddenly felt apprehensive? Is it possible you were picking up the energy from a classmate who didn't study?

I think we all are, at one time or another, energy vampires. We give off energy, and many times, we do it without our knowledge. It happens. Those around you can pick up that energy. It can merge with their energy and alter them in some way. If you are happy, just being there can make others happy too. The same is true if you are sad or annoyed or excited. The same can be said for others around you, others in the bus, on the subway, in the mall or anywhere else people get together.

For me, energy vampires are people who intentionally or not (and many times I believe the "or not" is true) sap your energy. They drain it from you, leaving you weak and vulnerable. They send out their energy – it mingles with yours – and returns to them. If you are happy and they aren't, their negative energy pulls your joy away from you and helps relieve them from their sadness. If they are anxious, the calmness you felt may soon give way to unexplained jitters.

If you have never felt anything like this, then you may want to do the journey just to learn the technique. If you said, "Ah-ha," as you read, drop the last "may" I said and just do it. I don't worry if this journey is too difficult for you because you are still in the early stages of learning. If you ask, and your guide says no or does something else with you, it's just not the right time. In a week or month, ask again.

The following items are my facts because they are true for me. But I have explained the difference between fact and opinion, and I know what is true for me is not true for everyone. Hence, they are only my opinions.

- I believe that we are in control of what happens to us on an energetic level.
- I believe that no energy, even from parents or friends, should enter us without our knowledge and permission.
- I believe that we each have the power not to allow any energy to enter us.

Now that I have told you my opinions, let me explain what I want you to do in Journey 9.0. You will need to do an additional journey, 9.1, as soon as you can after completing 9.0.

Please have a paper and pencil handy. You may wish to draw something as soon as you return to our reality.

Intent of Journey 9.0

Announce to Spirit that, from this day on, you do not give any outside energy permission to enter your body or energy field.

Say to your guide, "Show me a symbol that I can use to protect myself against outside energy wanting to enter my body or my energy field, and show me how to activate the symbol when it is needed."

When you meet your guide, tell her or him that first you want to announce something to spirit. Along with your declaration, ask your guide to relay the message to all the spirit guides she/he can. Then shout out, in your mindself, "I (say your first name) do not give any outside energy permission to enter my body or my energy field, now or in the future." You can repeat that as often as you or your guide feel is necessary. You can shout it to the trees, the distant mountains and the clouds. You can go far out into space and call out your message to the sun, moon and planets. You can go deep into the ground and call out your message in the darkness, if that is what you see. Tell whatever you see or sense in the spirit world around you that you do not give any energy permission to enter you. Jump to a mountaintop and shout it. Stand in the middle of the desert or on an ocean wave and shout it. Feel the energy within you as you are declaring your freedom from outside energy ever entering you again. (It is not a bad idea to repeat this journey whenever you feel it is necessary.)

Take a deep breath, not only with your mindself but also with your bodyself, and remember the energy of your voice. Feel the ultimate power/energy you used to announce to the spirit world that you do not give any energy or force permission to enter you or your energy field. Remember that feeling so you can recreate it in our reality if and when you need that extra push to make sure all outside energy obeys your will.

Feel what you say in your bodyself. Feel chills or tingles racing down your arms or back or chest. Involve your bodyself in this one journey. Hug yourself in both the spirit reality and in our reality. Believe in both realities that you have refused any energy from entering you.

Whether you call out to spirit once or twice or twenty times, it is up to you. Your emotional self will be raw and intense, and you may even feel the heat of your power in your bodyself as well. And when your emotions calm and you are fully aware that your spirit guide is there, next to you, waiting for you to finish, you'll know this part of the journey is done.

Now, ask your guide for a symbol that she/he can give you, that will help protect you when you need that protection and outside energy is trying to enter your body or energy field.

If your guide shows you a geometric shape, let's say a circle with crisscrossing lines (or any other shape), before moving on, study that shape. If you have to, apologize to your guide, ask her/him to wait for you, open your real eyes and draw the shape as quickly as you can. Then close your eyes and imagine yourself right back next to your guide. She/he will be there. Now state the next intention: Show me how to activate the symbol.

Many people have symbols of protection. Usually, they are closed shapes. They can be eggs, walnuts, crystal spheres or music boxes. The list can go on and on. Activating those kinds of symbols is kind of obvious. Imagine yourself within that closed shape and the outside energy just bouncing off it. If this is the case and you recognize the symbol, you do not have to break the journey and draw it, but just continue by asking how do I activate the symbol? What do I have to do to make the symbol work, to allow the symbol to prevent any outside energy from entering me? Please do this even if it is obvious.

When you are completely satisfied you know how to activate it, thank your guide and return to our reality.

I'd like you to do the next journey as soon as you can after you finished this one.

FYI: If you wish to do both 9.0 and 9.1 as one journey, please do so. When I did this journey, I only did one because everything was moving at a rapid speed, I was on a roll and I didn't wish to stop. Raccoon was with me and I knew as long as he was there, everything was just as it should be. If you can do the same, fine. If you need the break, also fine.

Journey 9.1

Energy Vampires, Part 2

You have a symbol that is yours and yours alone. You also know how to activate it. Next time you enter a space and just feel different from the way you felt a moment before, think of your symbol, active it the way you were taught, and concentrate on the activated symbol until you feel the way you used to. Mine, by the way, is a gazebo surrounded by light and I always imagine myself inside it. The light either acts as a protective wall to keep outside energy away or absorbs that energy, altering it until it becomes harmless. Either way, the energy does not enter me. The stronger the outside energy is, the brighter the light surrounding me. Your symbol can be anything your guide showed you.

Again, you have two intentions for this journey.

Intent of Journey 9.1

Journey to the middle world (that's the one we live in) and place that symbol in all the places you visit on a regular basis.

Ask your guide to create the symbol in front of you and bring it inside your body, leaving it there and instructing the symbol to activate itself automatically whenever it detects outside energy attempting to enter your body or energy field, even if you are unaware of that energy.

This will be your first middle world journey. Start this as you always have, meeting your guide at the usual place. Say to your guide that you wish to put your power symbol in all the places you regularly go to in your world, especially places like school or where you have ever felt any previous energetic loss. Ask your guide to come with you.

From within your journey, imagine yourself in your own

room. That's easy. See your mindself taking the symbol and putting it on the 4 walls. If it's a shape, slap your spirit hand against the wall and when you remove it the shape is where you put it. If it's an object, like an egg, imagine one in your hand and stick it on the wall with spirit Velcro. Then flying, because it is the fastest way, put the symbol on the outside walls of your house or the front door of your apartment. Appear in your classroom and do the same, going to all the rooms you have classes in (don't forget the gym, auditorium, and cafeteria and the hallways).

Then think of all the other places you regularly go to, malls or movie theaters, restaurants or places you hang out with your friends. Put the symbol anywhere you can think of, and each time you place it anywhere, repeat what you called out to spirit. "I do not give any outside energy permission to enter my body or my energy field, now or in the future." All this shamanic work is to add strength and power to help you keep energy you don't want away from you. Those symbols will be invisible to everyone else, and even to you most of the time. But they will appear if you choose to see them in case you need that ounce of extra protection. They will be there, in our reality, and you don't have to journey to see them. Just squint your eyes a bit and imagine them. You know they are there because you and your guide put them there. Your symbol is from spirit and it will be there for you, helping you whenever you need it. When you are done and have placed the symbol in all the places you can think of, ask your guide to return with you to the spirit world.

Now ask the second intent. Ask your guide to create the symbol before you. Ask her/him to please take that symbol and place it somewhere inside of you. Ask your guide to instruct the symbol to activate itself if it ever senses outside energy is attempting to invade your space. Your guide should then take the symbol, enter you, and when she/he returns, the symbol will not be there. One more thing to do, and then you are done. Just like you asked your guide to show you how to activate your symbol, ask now to be shown what will happen (how will you know) when the symbol activates itself. Then thank your guide and return to our world.

When I asked Raccoon to show me how the gazebo he left inside me would activate itself, I imagined a New Year's Eve paper horn. It's the one where you blow into it and the paper unwraps itself, making a noise as it does. I saw my gazebo popping out of me. It was at the end of the paper. I thought it kind of silly, but it worked. Even if your way is also silly, trust it.

Did it work for me? Yes. There were times when I was in a crowd and suddenly, while my real eyes were open, my mindself saw, I sensed, I thought about, the paper horn popping out of me. When that happened, I just concentrated on the gazebo's light surrounding me and repeated to myself, "I do not give you permission to enter me."

Another way I later found out was, and this might work for you also, sometimes instead of seeing or sensing my gazebo pop out of me, I just thought of it. The thought popped into my head as I entered a room or bus or any crowded space. The thought of my gazebo was in my conscious mind and I did not put it there. Whenever that happened, I never hesitated. In my mind, wherever I was, I activated my noise-making gazebo coming out of me and surrounding me in its light. I even let out a quick breath to imitate blowing the paper horn and at the same time, blowing any incoming energy away from me. Remember, I believe many times people are not aware of how they suck energy out of us and I may not be an intended target. Who was trying to invade my space wasn't important. I protected myself with my imagery as I imagined my gazebo surrounding me with light. I may not have known why I needed that protection, but I didn't stop to look around or question spirit. I just automatically protected myself. I trusted spirit. And now, you can do the same thing with your symbol, whatever it is, whenever you need it.

FYI: These shamanic concepts have many other uses that have nothing to do with energetic protection. These uses will be explained in future journeys. Therefore, if you have the time and the inclination please do Journeys 9.0 and 9.1 as soon as you can.

Journey 10

Travel to Your Future to
Help Solve Today's Problems

Earlier in this text I told you I'd explain how going back to your past or ahead into your future could help you a great deal in your present. Let's begin that by going into your future.

Time. We think of time as linear – a line with three words on it:

Past   **Present**   **Future**

The three are separate, and only in a writer's imagination can they meld into each other or can a person travel from one to the other and back again.

I'm going to give you a simple analogy of how shamans and shamanic practitioners think of time. Imagine a curtain covering a window that is made up of three large pieces of cloth. Imagine yourself standing in front of it, and with a magic marker, you write the word past on the first panel, present on the second, and future on the third. As long as that curtain remains closed, the panels representing the three times are separated. That's linear time. This is the way we view time. Now see yourself opening the curtain. What happens to the three times? The past panel touches the one marked present, the present touches future. And it is even possible for the future to touch the past. As long as the curtain is open, the past, the present and the future melt into each other. It is impossible to see where one time period ends and another time begins. This is shamanic time. It is non-linear time where past, present, and future all touch each other, allowing a shaman practitioner (that's you) to move from one time period to another very easily.

I should have told you that before you read this, ask your

intellectual self to take a break. It may be difficult for you to process what you read with that self. But since I didn't, let's take the next journey. If your emotional self accepts it, when intellectual self objects, which it may, you can just tell it everything is under control.

I want you to think of a problem you are currently having at this time in your life. Try not to make it a major problem. I say this because you're still learning how to react within a journey, and to question the guides you see while in their reality. I think you may have to converse more in this journey than you have in previous ones. So don't make it a life-changing problem. It ought to be some situation that you have been trying to resolve and, so far, you have not been able to. Not knowing what to wear for an upcoming event is not acceptable.

Intent of Journey 10

Ask your guide to take you to your future self after the problem you are having has been solved. Find out from that self how she/he solved the problem.

YOU MUST INCLUDE A TIME FRAME FOR YOUR GUIDE. How far in the future after the problem was solved do you wish the guide to go? You do not want to leave it up to your guide. If you do, you could find yourself visiting you when you are 50 years old and have forgotten the problem ever existed. Spirits are playful and will do things like that. If you ask your guide why she/he did that, the answer may just be, "You told me to take you to a future self after the problem was solved and I did." So decide on a time frame. It can't be too soon after the problem was solved because you want to know that it didn't reoccur. My suggestion would be three months after you solved the problem.

Now, since this is the first time you are time traveling, you have to keep the following in mind. In the beginning, the person you are going to, even if it is you, does not know who you are. Wouldn't you be a bit scared if someone just appeared in your bedroom, more so if that person looked exactly like you? First, tell the future self who you are and why you are there. That future self will know that you are beginning to do shamanic work, but you can remind her/him if needed. Simply tell your future self the problem and say why it is important for you to solve it in YOUR present.

Dialog with that future self. Ask any questions you have to. My suggestions are:

- What did that future self do that you haven't?
- Why did that self do those things?
- What happened and did anything unexpected happen?
- What steps did the future self take in your reality to help solve the problem?

If you are not sure about doing one or two of those steps, talk to the future self about them, express your concern and discuss other options. Ask questions, as many as you need. Have a real conversation. Remember, you have all the time in the world. You will be done when you have a plan on how to tackle the problem.

If you selected a problem that involves things that you can't control and your future self says there was no resolution (you were never able to transfer out of the worst math class you ever took with the worst math teacher you ever had), then focus the conversation on how did she/he cope with the situation. If you can't fix it and have to live with it, you might as well know how to cope better than you are now.

When all is finished, thank your future self. Don't forget to thank your guide too before you end the journey. She or he will be with you, so if you get stuck on what to say, ask your guide.

I hope that some information you received in this journey allowed you to think of a solution you hadn't thought of before, or a plan of action that might help. You should also know that you could use this technique whenever you need to. The future holds many keys for us and each key opens its own door. (I remind you it is a good idea to write down your journeys. If what your future self said made sense or if it gave you new ideas of what you can try, write them down.)

But this is important to know. When you journey to a future self, and you get your answer, that answer is for that day only. If you journey to your future self with the same problem the following day or week, you may get a different answer. The reason is the answer you received was based on the actions that the future self expects to happen. Don't forget that spirit always follows its free will rule. It doesn't dictate to us. You will not know all the actions that your future self expects to happen in order for the same outcome to occur. Your current actions, and the actions you do to solve the problem, may or may not be the same as your future self expected. You are the only one who can dictate what you will do in your near and far future. Your future self can only give you answers based on her/his perceptions of the past and the actions she/he expects to have happened in that past. But THAT past is YOUR present. If your present actions don't agree with the future self's perceptions of the past, if you do something different from what a future self expected, the outcome may be different from what you received in your journey. The only way to find out is to take several journeys and ask lots of questions.

Let me give you an example. In 6 months, you will be old enough to get your driver's license. But your parents have said that if you want to drive, you have to drive your own car (which you don't have) and pay all the expenses (which you couldn't because you have no job). You journey to your future self. You know your parents will not buy you a car, but you want to know what you can do so they will let you borrow their car on occasion.

After talking to your future self you found out that your parents did lend you the car because they realized how responsible you had become. That gave you an idea. Your plan of action how to soften your parents' minds between now and license time was to do everything possible to show them how responsible you really can be. You are excited about the idea of getting to borrow their car so you sit at your desk and write down all the things you want to do to show your parents they could trust you with it. In your excitement, you forget to do a family chore, putting the garbage on the curb for the morning pick up. Next day, you get yelled at because it will be three days until the next pick up. If you were to journey again that night, the answer you receive may not be the same as the previous day.

Therefore I would suggest you repeat any journeys to your future self because the information you came back with on that first journey may no longer be valid. You may have to change your plans several times in order to be able to drive that car.

Spirit sometimes writes the answers to your journeys on fog, and fog moves with the wind. Did I tell you that working with the spirits can sometimes be very frustrating? I'm sorry if I didn't.

Journey 11

Journey to Your Higher Self

If I told you all the questions you wish to ask spirit and all the answers you wish to hear were within you right now, would you believe me? I don't think so.

But I believe they are. I believe those answers are locked up in a part of us that I call our higher selves. For me, the higher self is that all knowing, all surrounding force that allows us to be part of (to be one with) everything in the Universe, to have a sense of morality so that we never have to question or ask if something we do is right or wrong. We know the difference; it's just that many times we choose to ignore what we know. The higher self is that part of us that was born when we took our first breath and remains solidly within us for our entire lives. It knows us better than we know ourselves. It knows why we are the people we are. It knows the reasons we do all the things we do, both good and bad. There is nothing about us the higher self does not know.

Some people refer to that force as divinity, God, a force that lives outside us and seeks to have us hear its messages. I believe that the force lives inside us. It is the God within us. I believe that force is aware when our actions are not in harmony with our environment, and I include in my definition of environment not only your reactions to the people around you, but to all that this world holds. I also believe that the higher self will not interfere with our free will choices. It will not stop us; it will not prevent us from doing all that we want, whether good or ill, to ourselves, to others or to the world we live on. It may whisper to us when it feels we are on the wrong path; but usually, its whispers go unheard by our conscious minds.

You have just journeyed to your future self. I want you to continue your journeys of self-discovery by journeying to your higher self. But before you start, you have to think of the question you wish to ask, and you may ask anything you wish about yourself. Why you are the person you are or why can't you seem to be the person you want to be? Why you do or don't do certain things? How can you change certain aspects of yourself that you wish to begin changing or how can you strengthen a part of yourself that you know needs that extra push?

I want you to really think about this. If you don't do all your assignments in school or wait until the last minute to do them, and they are poor because you rushed, you could ask your higher self why you aren't a better student. But you could also ask a question that will give you more information. Why am I lazy? Why do I procrastinate so many times?

I mentioned earlier that asking the right question is important. Though you can visit your higher self (or inner self – that word is also perfectly acceptable and means the same) as often as you'd like, forming the right question can be a great help. Since it should relate directly to an issue concerning you, I hesitate suggesting one.

Without selecting an intention for your journey, I can give you some general guidelines that might help you get the information you are looking for. You can start by thinking about any one of these:

- Why do I do (or don't do) something?
- Why do I behave in a certain way? Think of your personality traits – too shy, too selfish, too lazy, too pessimistic or optimistic, too nervous, too worrisome, too needing the approval of others or too not caring at all what anyone thinks. Maybe instead of too much of the trait you selected, you think you have too little of that trait and you wish to strengthen it. That's fine, too. Anything about you that you want more information about is a good topic for the higher self.

- What is the one thing that I can do that will let me – be happier – be freer – be not so much of (something you name) or be less of (something you name)?

Once you have the question, then you need to know what you wish to find out about it. Some of those questions that you might wish to follow up with are:

- When did I start being that way?
- Why did I start being that way?
- Why do I continue being that way?
- What is stopping me from being the way I wish to be?
- Can you show me what my life will be like when I have become the person I want to be?
- What are the first 2 steps in my reality that I can do to begin changing from the way I am to the way I wish to be?

I give you one more suggestion. Did you ever say to yourself, "What's wrong with me?" Whatever you thought was wrong, that is what you have to ask your higher self.

Once you have decided on the question, do the journey. Have a conversation with your higher self. Ask the follow-up questions I suggested or ask your own or a combination of both. And if there is too much for one journey, do two.

FYI: I told you once that you should not have any expectations when you take a journey. This is especially true for this one. I believe our higher selves are ethereal. They are ghost-like, having no defined shape. Because of this, there is no telling how the higher self may appear to you. It could be in a shape that you recognize and will be able to relate to. But don't expect it to resemble you or be a mirror image of yourself. It could be anything. If the higher self appears as a foggy mist or a bright light, you may have trouble relating to it. To avoid this problem, tell your guide to ask the higher self to appear in a human form.

If you still need help in forming your question ask your guide, either in a separate journey or before you ask to be taken to your higher self.

After completing the journey, if you need help in translating what you learned into actions in our reality, take an additional journey and ask your guide to help with deciding on a plan of action.

Intent of Journey 11

Ask your guide to take you to your higher self. When the higher self appears, tell her/him why you have come. Ask your question or questions. Then stay and have a conversation.

I hope that after you have completed this journey, you will have a deeper understanding of who you are, of what makes you the person you are. Your higher self can be one of your most important allies in the spirit world. That self knows you and what makes you special. It holds most of the answers you will ever need to know. But unlike guides who come and go for reasons we will never understand, if you want to ask your higher self a question, you have to decide to journey to her/him before you journey. They tend not to appear on their own.

Lessons Learned 2

Before you read this, take a moment to think about these last few journeys. Can you extrapolate (generalize what you learned in one area so you can apply that knowledge in a different area) any information that you can use in your shamanic future? I'm doing this so quickly after the last Lessons Learned because you may not realize how much knowledge the techniques you learned hold.

_____

_____

_____

Finished? OK, here's my opinion. In your journeys, you experienced the following for the first time.

You know the power and have felt the energy of your own spiritual voice. You have transferred that energy from the spirit reality to our reality. You not only claimed your power (by announcing that you refuse to allow outside energy to enter you) but you used it to dictate a future you chose for yourself. Never underestimate the strength and power of your affirmation of something you want. This does not mean spirit will give it to you, but if you are willing to do the work to achieve your goal yourself, spirit will support you completely. The possibilities for using this technique are many.

Suppose you are working on a fear you have. Proclaiming to the spirit world you will no longer be afraid is a major start. By experiencing the energy connected with not being afraid in the other reality, when that fear arises in our world, recalling the energy when you weren't afraid may be a huge boost in helping you overcome your fear.

Imagine you have to speak in front of your class and hate that with a passion. What if that were to happen tomorrow, and tonight you declare to spirit you will not be afraid. Within both realities, you feel the energy that surges into you as you make that declaration. Do you think that recalling and feeling that same energy pouring into you again just before you stand and walk to the front of the room might help you?

This technique, feeling energy from the spirit reality and bringing that energy back with you, can be used for journeys you haven't even thought about doing yet. Energy within us can stir up and affect your emotions and actions. Feeling the power of the energy associated with what you wish to accomplish may be a great help in actually accomplishing what you want.

You asked for and received a power symbol that would help protect you from outside energy. If you can imagine it, you can journey for it. There is nothing stopping you from asking for additional symbols for different circumstances. In the example I just gave you, what if you asked for a symbol to give you that extra courage to give your speech without faltering. What if, in that journey, you planted that symbol all over your classroom and even drew a small picture of it on the top of your speech notes or had an actual object in your pocket. What if, as you walked towards the front of the class, you squinted your eyes just a bit and imagined seeing your symbol surrounding you on the walls, desks, even on the wastebasket. If you feel the energy of your courage and allow your mindself to see the spirit symbol YOU placed all over the room, do you think that might help you to overcome your fear?

You journeyed to a future self in order to solve a present problem. You journeyed to your higher self in order to understand yourself better. Getting to each self should have been simple, and hopefully, you were successful in both journeys.

By taking what you learn from one journey and applying it to a different situation, you increase your knowledge. We each have within us what I call a basket of knowledge. And for each topic, subject or aspect of your life, you have a different basket. All that you have learned about shamanism is in your shamanic basket.

As you get older and more experienced, you will learn how to mix the items in your basket to increase your knowledge.

Personally, I think you have learned a lot, and even if some of your journeys were not successful, I think you should be very proud of what you have accomplished. But what I think doesn't matter. It's what you think that's important.

Journey 12

Merge with a Force of Nature

Intent: Imagine yourself in front of a force of nature. Ask the force for permission to merge with it and to teach you how to use its power and/or energy in our reality.

You have completed several heavy journeys and it's time for a break. This will be a simple one, and I hope you'll have fun with it. But it has a real purpose and I'd like you to try and remember it during your journey.

You are going to journey to a force of nature. If you wish your guide to join you, ask her/him to take you. If you wish to go solo, as soon as you reach the lower world, imagine yourself approaching the force you wish to be with. You may go to any natural occurrence you wish. It may be a river or a stream, gentle or rapids. It could be an ocean, calm on a sunny day or turbulent as in a summer storm. It could be the snow of an avalanche or an erupting volcano. It could be the wind, from hurricane to gentle breeze or a tornado whirling over landscape. It could be a cloud, white and fluffy or heavy with rain. It could a forest fire or the earth itself, shaking in an earthquake. Earth, air, fire, water – pick an element and a natural occurrence within that element.

Or, you could just ask your guide, which is never a bad idea. If you would like to do that, you have to change the intent. When you see your guide, say "Take me to a force of nature whose power and energy I need in my life now." You might love to be the tornado, but spirit may say that you need to learn the peace and calmness of a cooling early morning summer rain. When you are ready and see the force of nature you or your guide has chosen, ask permission to merge with it.

What should you do once you are within the force? Be one

with it. Feel the power that force can unleash or the gentle restraint it shows as it moves. The slow moving river uses the same energy that later on will explode into rapids. The energy of the countless waves that melodically travel in harmony with each other as they gracefully cross the ocean could suddenly become the overpowering force of a tsunami. Remember the one that took so many lives and created so much destruction in Japan.

Each elemental occurrence controls forces that can be anywhere from the softest of gentle to the most severe and destructive. Be that force. Ask it what it wishes to accomplish? Ask how the energy you are feeling from within it is helping to accomplish the task? Ask why the task needs to be accomplished?

Using power wisely is a major attribute. The wind cannot be strong all the time or crops would never grow. The current in the river cannot be at rapid strength all the time. How would the animals drink? How would the fish survive? All nature is in harmony with itself, even though we have no idea what harmony a hurricane can bring.

Whatever you (or your guide) selected, merge with it and be one with the power. Feel the energy, taste it, bring it into your bodyself like you did when you declared your intention not to allow outside energy into you. Allow your emotional self to fly or swim or just revel in being part of nature. Experience the experience.

Now, and this is important, say to the force that you are one with, "Show me how to use this energy safely and wisely in my reality, in my world. Show me how it can help me in my life now." This is major. There are teachers and lessons all around us. I told you spirit guides will eventually be your teachers and the force you are part of now is one of them. Learn from it, but you have to ask or else the lesson may be wasted. If you decide not to ask the question now, that's OK. But do the journey again and then ask. Or talk to your guide either after you leave the force or in your next journey. Don't allow the lesson to be wasted. When you have imagined all that the force of nature had to tell you, thank it and gently, even if you are within a tornado in the middle of its destructive cycle, disengage. Find your guide if she/he came with you, and if not, return to your bodyself on your own and slowly come back to our world.

FYI: In Journey 6, Dismemberments, I told you in my FYI to remember what it felt like during the journey. I ask you to do that again now. This journey was a 'feeling' journey. Ask yourself what did the energy feel like when you were part of the force of nature? Did the force of nature change from one aspect to another (a gentle rain became a thunderstorm) during the journey? If so, did the energy you experienced also change? Can you recall both? Now, can you think of any time in your life that if you had those same energetic feelings within you, it might have helped you in some way? Do you think recalling that same energy might help you in the future?

Journey 13

Travel to Your Past to Help Solve Today's Problems

Intent: Ask your guide to take you to a past self and ask that past self to remind you of something that you need to know now, in your present life.

I don't believe it is necessary to repeat information you already know or tell you how to do something you already can. What I wish to do is continue to open your mind to possible journeys that can help solve whatever problems life presents you with. Journeying to a past self can be a powerful journey and fits into that category.

The problem you may have with this type of journey is your youth. I don't mean being young is a problem. I mean that because so much of your past is recent to you (depending on your age), your past self may not have a lot to say about things you don't know or remember. Don't forget you journey to retrieve information that you can use in your present. The younger you are, the less relevant this type of journey may be. But knowing that your past self is available to you is another powerful tool you should put into your shamanic basket.

My instructions are simple. When you meet your guide, say that you want to go back to a past self when something occurred that you no longer or vaguely remember and remembering it will help you in your present life. My hope is that after the journey you will have that "Ah-ha" moment when the light bulb goes off in your head and you realized something you didn't know a minute before. If you learn nothing in this journey, which may happen, don't worry. I said the younger you are, the less relevant this may be. But the opposite is also true. The older you are, the more relevant this journey can be.

Don't forget to do the same thing you did in the beginning of Journey 10, journeying to a future self. Tell your past self who you are and why you are there. Then, state the intent and see what happens.

Major FYI
True or False

The example I am going to use in this FYI has to do with the last journey. But it relates to an issue that is at the heart of shamanism. It is that important. That's why it has its own section heading.

I am sure you all said to yourself in the beginning, "Is shamanism real or is it my imagination." I told you it doesn't matter. Both come from the same place within us. Now, I'm going into another concept and, to keep it simple, I'm just going to call it true or false.

I told you that spirit wishes to help us. Spirit will guide us in strange ways that we may not understand, but never doubt spirit's intentions are always for our higher good.

I'm going to make up a story about what is happening in your life and how you can learn from your past self. But I'd like you to see if you can't draw any connections between my made-up example and your real life.

You have always been uncomfortable or afraid of being in the water. Not the shower or tub, but the ocean, a lake, or even a swimming pool. Now, at 15 years old, you want to learn how to swim.

Your parents have arranged for private swimming lessons at the local pool. The closer the day to the first lesson comes, the more anxious you are. When your parents ask how come you are afraid, you answer, "I don't know. I guess it's just the way I am."

Pretend you journeyed to your past self. You asked that self, "Why I am so afraid of the water?"

A 3 year old answered, but not in a 3 year old voice – in your present voice and with your present maturity. (This is not a made-up 'what if' because that's just the way it would really work.) "I fell into the pool last week. I nearly drowned and had to go to the hospital. I'm never going into the water ever again!"

You said thank you to your past self and returned. Now, you ask your parents, your older siblings, your aunt and uncle, and all the other long-time friends of your family, especially those who knew you when you were 3 if you ever fell into a pool. They all said no. It never happened.

What spirit told you wasn't true. It lied and everyone who remembers you as a 3 year old confirmed the lie. You never fell into a pool. You never even fell in the bathtub.

I told you in the beginning of the book that real or imagination, it didn't matter. What matters is what you believe and how you react. In my example, we both know what would happen if you didn't believe what your past self told you. You wouldn't do anything about the issue and everything would stay the same. If you didn't believe you were afraid of water because you fell into a pool when you were 3, then your fear of water must really be from someplace else. I suggest you would say it came from the "I don't know why I'm afraid. I guess it's just the way I am." What do you think will happen when the day of your swimming lesson arrives? I suggest you aren't going to go.

Real or imagination, it doesn't matter. What matters is what you believe and how you react. To that statement, I am now going to add, true or false, it doesn't matter. What matters is what you believe and how you react.

Pretend you accepted what your past self said and never bothered to substantiate it with your parents. What if you didn't care if it was true or not? What if you accepted the truth of the statement, "I fell in the pool..." and just reacted as if it really happened?

In this second scenario, as the day of your swimming lesson approaches, you might say to yourself, "Why should I be afraid of the water just because I fell into a pool when I was 3? I'm not 3 anymore. I'll have a swimming instructor in the water with me. I won't go into any water over my head. I can't drown."

Using some of the techniques you have learned, you journey to retrieve a power symbol that would assist you in getting over your fear of water. You plant that symbol in the pool area and feel the energy within you when, during your journey, you experienced swimming. You bring that energy back with you and know you can recall it when it is needed. You could also add in the beginning of that journey, shouting to spirit, as you did before, that you are no longer going to be afraid of the water.

If you did that journey and knew that your guide would be with you when you went for your first lesson, do you think you would have gone to the pool and made an attempt to enter the water? If you recalled the energy you associated with swimming in the spirit world and brought it into your bodyself, would that help you get closer to the edge of the pool? If you merged with any aspect of water, and you recalled the energy you felt when being part of the water, do you think that would help?

Even if you didn't go in the water but just wet your feet on the first step leading down, wouldn't that have been a huge leap forward? Do you think that after one or two more journeys you might actually enter the water? If you followed this scenario, then you would have begun to solve the problem and begun to be less afraid of the water. But all this could only have happened if you accepted what your past self said about falling into a pool.

True or false, it doesn't matter. What matters is what you believe and how you react. The truths of spirit's statements are irrelevant. They don't matter. What matters is how you react to them. What matters is what you do in our reality. For me, in the shamanic world, true or false are the same, especially when spirit gives you information about your past in the hope that you may change something in your future. Yes, spirit told you that you almost drowned. Yes, it might not have been true in your reality. And yes, it didn't matter. What matters is what you do in order to overcome whatever you want to and you can't do that if you accept the excuse of "That's the way I am." If you accept that, you'll never change. But if spirit gives you another reason why you are the way you are in one aspect of your life, and you accept it and then do something about it, what difference does it make if what spirit said was true or not. The end result of spirit's lie was that you began to change something about yourself and move in a positive direction toward becoming the person you want to become.

In Lessons Learned 2, I gave you an example about being afraid to speak in front of your class. I pointed out how using what you learned in the Energy Vampire journeys might help. Now, using the same example, and adding to it, the journey to your past self, I want you to see why true or false is not important.

You journey to your past self or to your guide and ask why you are afraid of speaking in front of your class. The answer you get was when you were in the second grade, your teacher made a joke when you mispronounced a word and everyone laughed at you. (That happened to me because I used to say "wabbit" instead of "rabbit" and I think it was my third grade teacher who pointed it out, nice and loud in front of the class.) It might have happened to you but I doubt it. But let's just say you accept it. You react as if it were true. Aside from doing the journeys we discussed earlier, you reread your notes. You know what you are going to say. You are prepared. You remember that in the past when your classmates gave speeches, even if they weren't very good, the teacher never joked or made fun of anyone. That second grade teacher of yours is long gone. Might you say, "Isn't it silly of me to keep the joke the teacher made alive in my head for so long? I'm going to try not to be scared of standing in front of the class." Instead of overcoming a vague "that's the way I am," you now have a concrete reason why you are afraid. At your age, and based on the reason why you don't like to speak in front of your class, both your intellectual self and emotional self would realize that with a little effort, you can overcome your fear because YOU are no longer in the second grade.

To further explain this using my own past as an example, and to make a very long story short, in January 1995 my wife suddenly died of an aortic aneurysm. The aorta is the main artery leaving the heart and it carries blood to the rest of the body. An aneurysm is a bulge in an artery. When the bulge ruptures, the blood flow to the body stops – immediately.

That summer, feeling absolutely miserable, I took my first workshop in shamanism. I knew nothing about it except a major part of shamanic work involved healing, and if anyone needed healing badly, it was I.

It took a great deal of patience, and I thanked my teacher (Aimee Morgana remember) a hundred times, but finally, I began to journey. And when I did, I journeyed to make my life whole. I journeyed in order to change the person I was into the person I wanted to be. I took all the journeys I have suggested you take many times. I admit that in the beginning, I too asked, "Is it real or is it my imagination?" Do you know the expression "A light at the end of a tunnel"? It means that the end of 'something', usually an activity or project, is near. In the beginning, I couldn't even visualize the tunnel. But as I began trying to bring the things I learned from spirit into my world, I began to see myself grow. I began to take those very first, very little steps and they helped. I knew what I learned from my guides was my truth, my reality. It didn't have to be anyone else's truth. It was mine. And where did those truths come from? They came from spirit. When I could visualize that tunnel far in the distance, long before I saw any light at the other end, I knew that the positive outcomes of my journeywork, the slow changes I was going through to return myself to the land of the living, were the proof of spirit's realness.

I never asked if the information was true or not. I stopped asking was it real or my imagination because it didn't matter. Spirit told me what spirit told me.

I was exceedingly shy, and that was a major problem when I

wanted to meet someone that I could begin a new relationship with. Spirit told me that I was so afraid of people because of the actions of my brother when I was 1 or 2 years old and those actions continued through my very early childhood. What difference did it make if my brother really caused the shyness to begin? I reacted as if he did.

I did not believe very much in myself and had very little self-confidence. My journeys told me that the reason for my lack of self-esteem (self-confidence) came from not being fully supported or given any encouragement in what I did as a young child. What difference did it make if that really happened, if my parents or teachers never acknowledged something I did was really good. I reacted as if those things had happened.

I was so insecure that I wondered why I should bother to ask a woman out for coffee when she, of course, would say no. Spirit said I felt insecure because things in my early life seemed to come and go and I had no control over anything. What I wanted never mattered. What others wanted mattered more. What difference did it make if the examples spirit showed me in my journeys really occurred. I reacted as if they did. (I told you I needed major healing, didn't I?)

I knew that what had occurred in my past made me into the person I was (shy, no confidence, insecure). I also knew that those parts of my personality were with me most of my life. I accepted the "that's the way I am" and always thought there was nothing I could do about it. But once I believed the reasons behind my behavior and since those reasons were no longer present in my life, I knew that there was no excuse for me to be shy or lacking in confidence or being insecure unless I chose to remain that way.

When I said that's the way I am because THIS happened to me, I had that concrete reason for being who I was. Knowing the reason meant I could now work on a plan that would help me begin changing my life. It didn't matter if the actual reasons were true or not. What mattered was that I believed them and took steps to fix the problems based on my belief. What mattered was I no longer believed in "that's the way I am." I began to believe in "that's the way I WAS."

Please don't believe changing myself was easy. It wasn't. And changing something within you will not be easy either. It took a long time, many journeys, and many conversations with my guides. But the most of the shyness eventually left, the self-esteem slowly grew, and the insecurity was replaced with confidence in the person I was becoming.

The end result was my making major changes in my life. Spirit had to tell me what happened in a way that would give me the confidence to know that I could change what I had to, one step at a time, in order to become the person I wanted to be.

In my example of you and the water, your not being afraid to take those first lessons was what spirit wanted. But spirit had to present both of us with a specific reason why we were the way we were and in such a way that we would know we could overcome it. I said before, spirit gives you what you need. And now I add, spirit gives you what you need in a way that you can understand it and in a way that will allow you to achieve your goal. I reacted to what I learned in my journeys as if they really happened. And because I reacted as if they were true, I was able to grow and reclaim my life.

In my opinion, when spirit tells you something in order to help you achieve a goal you consider important, questioning the validity of the information is a waste of energy. All that matters is what you believe and how you react. But, I'd like you to think about what you just read and come to your own conclusions.

Journey 14

Go to a Part of Yourself

Intent: Go to your guide and ask her/him to create with you a very safe place. Then ask your guide to call in a part of your personality that your guide feels you need to talk to.

It's my belief that this type of journey is important for you to know because in my struggle to change myself, I used it many times. You may not have a great need for it now, but it is definitely the kind of journey you should put into your shamanic basket.

This kind of journey may be difficult because it may force you to look at a part of your personality that you may not wish to deal with. But the insight it will provide you with is worth much more than the effort you may have to put into it. This journey will allow you to look deeply into yourself in order to find out how you can begin to change a specific part of your personality that you (or your guide) think needs to change in some way. Since this will be your first attempt, I ask you to please trust your guide to select that part for you. In the future, you will tell your guide the part of you that you wish to meet.

How would you describe yourself? How would you describe your friends, people you admire or look up to? How would you describe people you don't like? The words you use to answer those questions are probably personality traits. Personality traits include the actions you do, the attitudes you have, and the behaviors you possess.

All people, including us, are made up of many different parts. If you are a caring person, you can't look at a news story about a family whose child was killed without feeling a little sadness. If you are an uncaring person, it's just another news story that has nothing to do with you. What are a few other opposites that people can be? They could be: considerate or inconsiderate, studious or lazy, selfish or unselfish, honest or dishonest, cooperative or uncooperative, friendly or unfriendly. The list can go on for another two pages.

Some parts of our personality we like, some parts we don't. Sometimes, the parts we like can be too strong or too weak within us. Sometimes the parts we don't like can be so strong that even though we don't like what they tell us to do, we do them anyway. Being afraid of water is an example of this. Even though you might have wanted to learn to swim very much, the part of you that kept your fear alive was so strong you had to give in to your fear. (You could have used this upcoming journey to make you aware of why you were afraid of water or to speak in front of your class. Instead of journeying to your past self, you could have journeyed to that part of you that is causing those fears. Would you have gotten the same answers? Only spirit knows that!)

This journey is a powerful way to compromise with the part of you that you wish to change. When you want to do (or not do) something in this reality, and a part of you whispers that the reason you act in a certain way (or don't act in a certain way) is because "that's just the way you are," that whisper will not be true. In this journey, you will begin to realize that the excuse, "just the way you are," is no longer acceptable and you are going to have to start changing the "who you are" into the who you wish to become.

Journey to your guide and say, "Take me to a part of myself (a part of my personality) that you think I should meet. I want that part to have a human form and meet it in a place where I will feel safe and secure." Go with your guide and when you reach that place ask the guide to get the part.

The person who will appear in your journey is a part of your personality, a part of yourself. You want that part to appear in human form because if you encounter an abstract form, a glowing light, or a non-human form, a dark cloud, large rock, anything like that, you may have a hard time relating to it.

Again, I am at a disadvantage not being with you after you return from the journey so we could discuss it. So let me make up a scenario and hopefully you can apply it to your own journey.

Suppose the body parts of the person before you are out of proportion. Her/his head and hands are much too large. Her/his chest is much too small. The first thing you have to do is ask what part of me are you? The answer is I'm Selfish. Since you asked your guide to choose the part, regardless what you think about that part of your personality (but I'm not selfish, you say to yourself) it is there for a reason. Trust that it is the part that you need to deal with now.

You must realize from the very beginning that whatever is before you, you CAN control it. You are uncomfortable looking at Selfish with its out of proportion body. Ask it to please become more like you want it to be. In this case, you ask it to increase the chest cavity and decrease the size of its head and hands. When it gets to be normal, tell it to stop. Remember – you can control the part you see – it does not have to control you unless you let it. Asking it to change its shape, even in the smallest way, will reinforce the idea that you are in control.

Next I want you to have a conversation with the part. Some of the questions you might want to have answered are:

- When did you start being so strong (or weak)?
- Why did you start being so strong (or weak)?
- Why are you so strong (or weak) within me now?
- What did you do for me in the past?
- What are you doing for me now?
- What do you want from me now?

You have to think carefully and quickly when you have this conversation because your goal is to have that personality part to become either less or more powerful. You don't want it to go away altogether because you need to be selfish in certain things. Your goal in this conversation is to strengthen (or weaken), depending on the part of your personality you journey to, the selfishness within you and you can do that in several ways.

How are you going to strengthen or weaken that part? These are some of my suggestions, but based on what is before you in your journey, you may have to change them. However, it is important that you keep in mind that you are going to have to reach an agreement with Selfish. The only way you can do that is compromise.

Thank Selfish for being with you, for teaching you the lessons it did, for being with you in the beginning when it protected you in some way. (This is important!)

Based on what the part said, explain that the reason for it being so strong (or weak) within you happened in the past and is no longer present in your life. Explain why you want it **not to be** the way it is. Explain how it is affecting your life in a negative way.

(Here, you have to think. Maybe some of your friends are pulling away from you because when everyone chips in money for something, you always put in the smallest amount. People are calling you cheap or stingy. Anything you say will help. In this case, emotional arguments can be very effective. Don't forget, you are talking to a part of yourself so emotions may be more powerful than logic.) Say whatever you have to, in order to convince the part that remaining as it is – is not in your best interest. (Ask your guide for help if you need to.)

Ask the part, and this is highly important regardless of the trait you are facing, what can we (Selfish and you) do together that will allow you to remain within me but let me be more (or less) selfish in my life?

Then you must also ask, what can I do in my reality that will satisfy and support you (the new Selfish) so you will keep the compromise you just agreed to and allow me to live a better life?

Remember, you have been speaking to a facet of yourself. That part of you really wants what's best for you. Usually, it started acting the way it is now in order to protect you from something earlier in your life. It will work with you. If you try, you can make the compromise happen!

Hopefully, you and Selfish will come to an agreement. Sometimes, taking several journeys and making small compromises each time may work better than making the one large compromise. It can be especially useful if you and Selfish can establish a friendly working relationship. An important thing to remember, aside from finding out the information I suggested, is before you end the journey thank the part for wanting to help you to live a better life.

When the part leaves, talk to your guide and discuss how you will do in the real world what you said you would, even if it is only one little step at a time. If you can't do everything, at least do some. Then journey back and have another discussion with the part. Be ready to explain why you didn't do everything you said you would. Stress what you did do and what you will continue to do.

You have to honor your word to Selfish. You have to honor your word to all who dwell in the other reality.

I did this journey many times as I was pulling myself up from the muck I was stuck in during the first few years after my wife died. I spoke to selfishness, ego, confidence, body image and several others. Remember I told you that if you can think of it, you could journey to it. The same is true with this type of journey. You can journey to any part of yourself that you need to get information from. You can do this journey whenever you need to. The procedure is the same; the questions will be the same. The only difference is you will ask your guide to bring you to the specific part you want to speak to.

After hearing from the part why it became the way it is in the first place, you could journey back to your past self to get more information about what was happening in your life at that point, if you don't remember.

FYI: Your guide wanted you to meet the part you just journeyed to. Do you think you needed to speak to that part? Why yes or why no? Now that you know you can journey to specific parts of you, what part of you do you think you should visit in the future?

Another FYI
Lose the Drum

John Perkins is a Western shaman who not only was one of my teachers, but also became a friend and colleague. He has written several books on shamanism as well as becoming a *New York Times* bestselling author writing books that are not on this topic. As a matter of fact, I used his definition of a shaman in the beginning of this book. He always told the following story at many of the workshops I assisted him in teaching.

Earlier in his life, John owned an alternative electric company in Florida. He said that many of the business decisions he made were based on shamanic journeys.

He told that story for a reason. When he was at a meeting (I think the example he used was meeting bank officials), he could not excuse himself before deciding on something they were discussing, take out his drum and do a shamanic journey. If he had done that, the only thing the bankers would have said was, "Close the door on your way out." So John took quick journeys without anyone knowing. He journeyed in a moment of thought, without drum or any music.

John wanted the participants in his workshop to be able to do the same. He wanted them to be able to do a journey anywhere, on a bus, train or plane, or sitting in an office waiting for their appointment time. (Not while driving a car!) He didn't want them to be tied to the sound of the drum.

When I journey now, I rarely listen to drums or music. The last journey wasn't my idea and neither was Journey 17. For Journey 14, I was sitting at my desk not knowing what to write. So I closed my eyes and went to my cave. Raccoon wasn't there; but instead of leaving, I looked around as I always do. I saw a pond. Like the void, whenever the pond is there, I dive in. I came out on a grassy plain like I always do, and there, sitting under a lone tree, was Lioness. I went to her. We walked together in the tall grass and I asked what she thought I should write about. The message I got from Lioness was to ask you to journey to a part of yourself. Before I could say that I had thought of that but decided it was too difficult for you, Lioness told me not to let you pick the part. Let your guide do it. I knew the rightness of that answer as soon as I heard it because your guide would not bring you to a part of yourself that you were not ready to meet, or one that you would not be able to work out some sort of arrangement to reach a compromise with. Then I thanked her, returned to my cave and opened my eyes. I needed neither drum nor music to take the journey.

I'd like you to do what John suggested to the people in his workshops: do not become dependent on drums or music or anything else. The next time you journey, I suggest you make some small changes. Instead of lying down, sit up in a chair. Instead of listening to music or a drumming tape, listen only to the sounds of the room. Instead of dimming the lights, leave them on. When you are ready, close your eyes and start. If you can't journey, then go back to the regular way and try doing it this new way later.

This is a wonderful addition for your shamanic basket.

Journey 15

Point of View, Seeing from Another's Eye

You ought to understand by now that shamanic journeying can be a great help in solving everyday problems. You should also realize that the more information you can gather about a problem, the greater the chance you have of solving it. Asking your guide to take you to the right place can be critical in finding out what you want in the easiest way possible.

You have journeyed to your higher self, to your past and future selves and to a part of your personality. All are valuable tools that you can call on countless times when you need to. The technique in this journey is to give you another way of getting as much information as possible about a problem you are having with another person without intruding on that person's personal privacy.

Very early on, I told you not to have any expectations about what will happen in a journey. Remember that when you start this one. Allow it to play itself out without judging what occurs while it is occurring. That means don't allow your emotional self to say things to you like, "That's not true or she/he is lying." Don't get emotional about what is happening. Wait until the journey is over. Then, you can either remain in the spirit world and discuss what you learned with your guide (a good suggestion if you have the time), or journey back to your guide and have that discussion later. Either way, when you are fully back in our reality, write down what you learned in your journal. This journey should not require any immediate action on your part. I want you to process the information you receive, and think about it carefully. Again, don't just assume you are 100% right and the other person is 100% wrong. You will experience what you will because your guide wanted you to experience exactly what you did. By this time in your shamanic career you are probably aware that your guides know what is best for you.

For this journey I'm going to suggest you select a person in your immediate family (sibling first, parent second) with whom you are having a disagreement. I have a feeling that a brother or sister may come to mind. If so, stick to a sibling.

Go to your guide and ask to see a problem (either a current or a recurring one, but state the problem to your guide) from the eyes of (person's first name) with whom you are having the dispute with. Then be open to whatever happens.

You may find that you are looking at yourself or that you are in a sibling or parent's room. You may just hear what the other person is thinking (in your own voice) about the issue you brought up. You may see yourself during an argument and hear what the other is thinking as you stated your points for your side of the discussion. It is impossible to tell what you will imagine in this journey because everyone will experience it differently. Just go with whatever happens. Don't judge it.

I have done this journey and usually found it helpful. I didn't ask questions during the journey but rather just went with whatever happened. Though I was still myself in the journey, my mindself was not speaking for me but rather for the other person. I was myself, but at the same time I wasn't myself either. I felt very discombobulated. That's why I didn't say much. Remember, you ARE NOT BECOMING the person. You cannot affect her/his behavior or her/his attitude in any way. Your guide will not allow you to invade a person's privacy if that is your goal.

In the issue you have brought up, you will feel you are correct and the other person is wrong. But the other person will feel exactly the same. This journey, this technique, will allow you to view the issue from the opposite point of view. I repeat, you ask your guide for help and whatever you experience is because your guide wanted you to be aware of it. You are not intruding in the other person's space. You cannot 'send a thought' to the other person asking her/him to change her/his mind. You cannot change their attitude. That's why I said don't get emotional. It is solely your journey and your guide is just supplying you with what you need most, information.

The ultimate goal, just as it was when you journeyed to a part of your personality, is to reach a compromise in our reality with the other person. You may have to give up some of your 100% being right and convince the other person to do the same. Since you are the shamanic practitioner, it may be up to you to begin a conversation with that other person and begin a dialog about solving the issue. If you feel you know some of the reasoning behind the other person's issue, then you might be able to suggest possible ways of accommodating each other. In the end, if you each give a little, you may both end up winning more than you have now. And if not and things remain the same, at least you tried.

Go ahead. Try the journey. You may not be ready to discuss what you learned with the other person. Don't worry about that. If you don't at this point, then keep your journal handy and broach the topic when you are ready.

FYI: What was the result of this journey? Did you gain an insight that you did not have before? Were you surprised with the point of view of the other person? Do you think that you learned something about yourself in this journey? If so, what?

Journey 16

Be an Animal

You have merged with a spirit guide and know how it feels to be one with her/him. You have merged with a force of nature and felt the power and energy that Mother Earth can use when she needs to. Now, I want you to do it on your own. When you reach the lower world, say to your guide, I want to shapeshift into an animal. Ask your guide what animal she/he suggests. (This is optional – you could also tell your guide which animal you wish to become. However, since this is the first time you are attempting this type of journey, allowing your guide to suggest one may be the most beneficial to you.) Then imagine your mindself changing you into that animal. If you can, feel the changes that are taking place in your bodyself as well as in the spirit world. Allow your bodyself to move as the animal during the changing process. Now, within the spirit world, be the animal. Use all of your five senses as the animal. When the change is complete call your guide.

Once you have become the animal, do whatever you wish. This is a fun journey so enjoy yourself. You have nothing to learn unless your guide hits you on the head and says, "Learn this."

I want you to experience your personal power in changing into the animal and in being the animal. I want you to feel the attributes of the animal. Feel its strength, its speed, its cunning, and its power. (This is another 'remember how it feels' journey.) And don't forget, all spirit guides are powerful, even a butterfly, a cricket, or a dove. I want you to do this because I want you to know you can, any time you want. Now, instead of merging with Wolf, you have the power to shapeshift into Wolf. When you do, you will be the wolf and all its attributes will be within you. If your guide selected the animal for you this time, it was because it may be important for you to experience its attributes at this point in your life. Next time, do it yourself. You can do it just for fun, as in this journey, or you can do it to feel the energy (characteristics) of the animal you need.

There is one more thing I want you to know. You can do this journey with the forces of nature too. Instead of merging with the tornado or river or cloud, you can shapeshift into them. You can become the force and feel its power and energy. If you wish to, do another journey and be a force of nature before you do Journey 17.

When you do this type of journey, REMEMBER this. When you merge with spirits, you feel their power and energy through them. When you shapeshift into a spirit, the power and energy of those animals (or forces) are created BY you. You are creating it in the spirit world and you can bring that power back to your world whenever you need it. In this past journey, you did not share the power of "Being an Animal" with your guide. You created it. You lived it. You were it.

Journey 17

Travel to Part of the World That Needs You

Well, you reached it – the last journey. Somewhere between the beginning of this book and this point, I stopped being your teacher. I passed that job over to your shamanic guides and they will do a much better job at it than I. I tailored this text to most of you, remembering how unsure I was when I started and the problems I had in my beginning. I tried to address the problems I thought you might have. I asked you to do journeys that would show you how to navigate the world of spirit. You know the different kinds of things to ask for. You know which of your guides might offer you the best and/or easiest understandable answers. You are now perfectly capable of continuing your shamanic work on your own and you can do that with complete confidence. I promised you something in the first paragraph in this text. I believe I have kept that promise. You now **are** a shamanic practitioner!

By continuing your relationship with your spirit guides and accepting the new ones that will appear, your future lessons will be tailored exactly for you. Your shamanic guides will tell you, show you, and suggest to you exactly what you need at that moment in your life. I can't do that. I never could because I don't know you. Your guides do.

If you have completed most of the journeys in this text, if you feel that you are a different person no matter how slight that difference may be, you have accomplished your goal.

There is a lot more to do and learn about accepting the role of a shaman in our Western culture and I hope you are committed to spending the time and effort in doing so. Shamanism is needed in our world. This last journey will give you an example of what I have just said.

Before I give you the details of that final journey, I'd like to say the following. It is my opinion about the role WE as shamans and shamanic practitioners can play in this world.

I think we should consider using our shamanic talents to do more than just improving our lives. We should use our skills to add to the greater good of the world community we live in. I think we should give back to spirit in any way we can for all that spirit has (and will continue to do) for us. I don't downplay improving yourself. At your stage in life, it is all I, and I am sure spirit, expect. During my first 5 or 6 years as a shamanic practitioner, improving myself was my only goal. All my time and efforts were spent in changing myself. When that change happened for me, as it will happen for you, I began to want more from the shamanic experience. It was only then I looked to the horizon to see what else spirit may hold for me. This last journey is a preliminary one given to you to explore the possibilities that may present themselves in your future, possibilities in an area where you can make a difference. If you choose not to do this journey, that's all right. This journey is optional. But I think many of you will do it and some of you may find it life changing.

Why? I told you this is not my journey and that the idea came from Raccoon.

Not sure of how to end this text, I journeyed and asked Raccoon, "What should the last journey be?" I went to my cave, and Raccoon was there, sitting on top of the rock. I joined him and we never left. I asked and he answered.

The more I thought about what he said, the more I believed in its rightness. I believe that Raccoon felt if you took this journey, you might realize something that you didn't know. You may find something that you might be able to do in order to bring a positive change to the global home you live on. You might make a difference. That's a heavy sentence, isn't it?

Imagine making a difference in the world. Making a difference doesn't mean you have to become a doctor and discover a cure for cancer. It could be the smallest of changes such as collecting magazines that you, your parents and their friends have read and donating them to a local nursing home or other facility. How does that change the world? Someone in that nursing home who has nothing to do but sit and stare at a TV might like to spend a few hours looking at those magazines. For those moments, the quality of that life may be improved. And every time the life of one person, one animal, and one tree is helped, then the world changes for the better. A million whispers may turn into a sound that can crack the foundations of the world. Wow! That's another really heavy sentence. But it is true.

Many times, people may never know the total effect they may have in creating that difference. When I was assisting John Perkins and Llyn Roberts during their many shamanic workshops at Omega Institute in upstate NY, before each workshop I went to a place near the edge of the forest. I stayed there for several minutes drumming to the spirit of the forest, the spirits of the trees. And as I drummed, my mindself said, "Please, let me make a difference in the lives of some of the people that I will meet." Sometimes those workshops had 60 people or more. I couldn't interact on a personal level with all of them. But I always interacted with some of them. Did I help them? I think so. Was it a long-lasting help? I hope so but, to be honest, I don't know. Could some of the people I met, after attending the workshop and using something they learned from me, go out and accomplish what they wanted? Again I think so. Could accomplishing what they wanted have had a positive effect in their communities, whether local community, state or national community, or global community? It could have. Did it? I don't know. I'll never know.

If you stand alone outside at night holding a candle, you are surrounded by darkness. If, by what you do, you can get another person to stand with you holding another candle, the darkness gets pushed back just a little. What if two more join you? What if four more join you? What if other people standing alone like you, because of what you did or started, join you? Soon, because of your actions, because of what you started, that light may spread over great distances.

You may not be able to change the world now. You're too busy changing yourself. But you can begin to think about it, and I think that was Raccoon's idea. He wanted to get you to think about something larger than yourself. I told you spirit could do nothing in our world remember? They need to find people to make the changes that they feel are needed and you just might be one of those people.

This is what I think Raccoon wants you to do. In this journey, find your guide and say you want to go to a part of the world that needs you. When you reach your destination, if you don't understand why you are there, which may or may not happen, ask your guide. If you think you know, discuss it with your guide. Then say you want to know how you can make a difference. Get as much information as you can. Is there anything that you, regardless of your age, can do? And if not now, when?

Once a day, every day, I go to a website, Freekibble.com. I read a multiple choice trivia question about dogs and select an answer. I then click on "Feed Cats" and do the same. Regardless if I am right or wrong, Freekibble.com receives a donation of 10 pieces of kibble every time someone clicks on an answer. It's not very much, is it, 10 pieces of dry dog or cat food? I do not know when you will read this, but from the time Freekibble.com started until today, August 12th, 2013, they have donated to various animal shelters around the United States over 11 million meals, or 1,846,124,650 (1 billion, 846 million, 124 thousand, 6 hundred and 50) pieces of kibble to homeless dogs and cats. And why do I mention it? An 11-year-old girl, Mimi Ausland, started that website.

Want to read more? I Googled, "stories about children that changed the world" and I clicked on the first listing I saw. The web address is: http: www.mnn.com/lifestyle/responsible-living/photos/8-amazing-kids-who-have-changed-the-world/get-ready. Those articles may or may not be available when you read this. If you are interested, you can always go to their home page, www.mnn.com and search their website. But, I'm going to tell you about two young people:

Ryan Hreljac was only 6 years old when he learned that many children in Africa had to walk over a mile just to collect fresh water and bring it back to their village. Ryan decided he wanted to build a well for a village in Africa. With the help of his parents, he began to raise money (by doing household chores and speaking to people and asking them to donate). Eventually, he collected enough money to build one well. Of course he didn't do that by himself. There were many adults who listened to him and stood next to him as he held his candle in the darkness. In 1999, at the Angolo Primary School in a northern Ugandan village, and because of one 6-year-old boy, that first well was completed. Since then, the Ryan's Well Foundation (www.ryanswell.ca), has completed 667 projects in 16 countries, bringing access to clean water and sanitation to more than 714,000 people.

In 2008, 9-year-old Katie Stagliano brought a tiny cabbage seedling home from school as part of the Bonnie Plants Third Grade Cabbage Program. She cared for her cabbage and eventually it grew to 40 pounds. Katie donated her cabbage to a soup kitchen where it helped to feed more than 275 people. Moved by the experience of seeing how many people could benefit from the donation of fresh produce, Katie decided to start a vegetable garden and donate the harvest to help feed people in need. Today, Katie's Krops (www.katieskrops.com/home.html) donates thousands of pounds of fresh produce from numerous gardens to organizations that help people in need. Again, Katie's candle came in contact with other candles and those candles were held by people who were older, loved the idea she came up with, and helped Katie's Krops grow into what it is today.

The purpose of this journey is not to come up with an idea that will change the world. It is to show you an area of the world that needs human intervention. And that area doesn't have to be on the other side of the world. It could be just around your block. It might be nothing more than a vacant lot you pass on your way to school. You might think that a community garden would be great. And if you can't do anything now, maybe in a year you might be able to. Maybe if you talked to enough people, your candle could join with others and a change might occur. If it doesn't, then you still will have made a difference because you tried. I believe that if one life is changed, so is the world. And the two examples above are to show you that you don't have to be an 'important adult politician' to start the change.

If, in your journey, you are taken to a different part of the world, and know that it may be years before you can do what spirit may suggest, then ask how can you use the knowledge you were just shown in your community? Who knows what may happen.

The intent of this journey is to travel to a part of the world that needs you. The purpose of this journey is to show you a possibility that might exist for you. If you wish to accept it, either now or in the future, that's up to you – free will remember? When you use the information you receive while in the shamanic world, it cannot hurt – but it could change the world or a very small part of it.

Conclusion

It's done. In the beginning you were curious. You talked it over with yourself and decided it was time to test your curiosity. As you read this book and completed the journeys, you began to walk the shamanic path. You stopped feeling silly when you journeyed and realized that being a shamanic practitioner could really help you in your everyday life. Maybe it didn't help all the time, but hopefully, it did some of the time. I hope you will continue walking this path because there are so many things you could do. There are also many more things to learn, areas that I have not even touched on.

I end this book by thanking you for following your shamanic dream. Whether you continue journeying on your own or stop now is not relevant. What you have learned will always be with you. Five years, ten years from now, the personal truths you will find within the shamanic world will still be there. They will always be there, waiting for you to come and seek the answers to your questions. Your excursions into the other reality have opened doors for you that you didn't even know existed before you picked up this book. You should now be filled with possibilities. If you can bring even a few of those possibilities into your world, your reality, your life, your home and your planet, Mother Earth will be better off because of what you will have accomplished.

One more thought – if you want to continue your shamanic work but find it difficult to decide what to journey on, you may wish to get "Shamanism: The Book of Journeys." I told you earlier that I co-authored that book with Dr. Eve Bruce. It is a reference book containing many different types of journeys. Like the journeys in this book, the ones in The Book of Journeys are all geared towards one purpose – to help you move your life from where it is to where you wish it to be in your future.

May You Always Walk with Spirit.

The Beginning

Soul Rocks is a fresh list that takes the search for soul and spirit mainstream. Chick-lit, young adult, cult, fashionable fiction & non-fiction with a fierce twist